Good Friday People

Good Friday People

SHEILA CASSIDY

Maryknoll, New York 10545

The Catholic Foreign Mission Society of America (Maryknoll) recruits and trains people for overseas missionary service. Through Orbis Books, Maryknoll aims to foster the international dialogue that is essential to mission. The books published, however, reflect the opinions of their authors and are not meant to represent the official position of the society.

First published in Great Britain in 1991 by Darton, Longman and Todd Ltd, 89 Lillie Road, London SW6 1UD and in the United States of America by Orbis Books, Maryknoll, NY 10545.

ORBIS/ISBN 0–88344–471–X

For my guides, philosophers and friends

John King MSC

Michael Ivens SJ

Jean Vanier

Bonaventure Knollys OSB

and for all those who have, in their different ways, walked with me along the road to Jerusalem.

Contents

Acknowledgements

This comes as a sort of public hug to all who have helped to make this book possible. First there is Morag Reeve and all at DLT without whose quiet faith I would never have been crazy enough to try and write a book in two and a half months. Then come my friends at Christ the King Retreat House in Syracuse, New York: Jim and Pete and Juan and Marlene and Frank who listened patiently to my first chapters and cheered me over the first hurdle.

I owe an enormous debt of gratitude to four people: Angela Tilby who read the first draft and advised me on the manuscript; Bonaventure Knollys OSB without whose love and knowledge of Scripture I would never have even begun to try to unravel the mystery of Jesus' death and rising; and Antony Keane OSB of Glenstal who showed me the icon of the Harrowing of Hell and gave me the Gospel of Nicodemus; last but not least come Benedict and Lila Ramsden who not only opened the door for me into the amazing world of Orthodox spirituality and liturgy but spent many patient hours helping me to clarify my ideas for the last few chapters.

My greatest thanks, however, must go to my Good Friday people: to the martyrs of El Salvador, two of whom, Ita Ford and Carla Piette, I am proud to call my friends; Suzi and Vince Lovegrove, Jane and Kevin Keary, Jimmy Doherty and to all those who would prefer to remain unnamed. Without their inspiration this book would never have been conceived, let alone written.

The very last hugs, however, go to Christine Costin and Barbara Tappy who have laboured late into the night deciphering and typing this manuscript.

SHEILA CASSIDY

Thanks are due to the following for permission to quote copyright material: Cairns Publications, from *Healing – more or less* by the Revd James E. Cotter; Carlyon-Gillespie Film Productions Pty Ltd, from *Suzi's Story*; Darton, Longman & Todd Ltd and Doubleday & Company Inc, from *The Jerusalem Bible*; Faber & Faber Ltd, from *'Choruses from "The Rock" '*, *Four Quartets* and *Murder in the Cathedral* by T. S. Eliot, and from *The Lenten Triodion* translated by Mother Mary and Kallistos Ware; HarperCollins Publishers, from *Uncommon Prayer* by Daniel Berrigan, and from *Holy the Firm* by Annie Dillard; David Higham Associates Ltd, from *Still Falls the Rain* by Edith Sitwell, and from *Our World* by John Harriott; International Committee on English in the Liturgy Inc, from *Rite of Holy Week;* Lutterworth Press, from *Archbishop Romero* by Placido Erdozain; Anna McKenzie, from her unpublished poetry; The Maryknoll Sisters, from *The Same Fate as the Poor* by Judith Noone; Orbis Books, from *The Voice of Blood* by William J. O'Malley, from *The Gospel in Solentiname*, volume 2, by Ernesto Cardenal, from *Archbishop Romero: Memories and Reflections* by Jon Sobrino, and from *Romero: A Life* by James R. Brockman; Reform Synagogues of Great Britain, from *Forms of Prayer,* volume 1, *Daily and Sabbath Prayerbook*; St Paul Media Productions UK, from *Theotokos*, 1989 Icon Book-Calendar; Richard Scott Simon Ltd, from *Night* by Elie Wiesel, copyright Les Editions de Minuit, 1958; SCM Press Ltd, from *Letters and Papers from Prison* by Dietrich Bonhoeffer; Sheed & Ward Ltd, from *A Rocking Horse Catholic* by Caryll Houselander; Stainer & Bell Ltd, from poetry by Sydney Carter; Veritas Publications, from *It's Never the Same* by James Doherty. Author and publisher would be glad to hear from any copyright holder whom they have been unable to trace, so that they can make acknowledgement in future editions of this book.

1

Introducing Good Friday People

It takes so much to be a full human being
that there are very few who have the
enlightenment or the courage to pay the price.

Morris L. West
The Shoes of the Fisherman

This is not a book for the faint-hearted, make no mistake of that. It is a book for Lent and as such it demands that the reader, like Thomas, put his or her hand right into the side of the crucified Christ.

It is, first and foremost, the story of a journey: the journey towards the Cross, and as such it tells the familiar story of Jesus of Nazareth; but, it tells too, in parallel inextricably intertwined, the story of those whom I call my Good Friday people: a motley group of saints and sinners mysteriously called to share in the sufferings of Christ.

Good Friday people is a term that I have coined to refer to the people who, for whatever reason, find themselves called to powerlessness and suffering. It is in some ways synonymous with the Hebrew word *anawim*, the little people, the marginated, disenfranchized ones, but it is broader than that, for it encompasses men and women from all walks of life who are called by name, summoned to climb *down* the ladder, to share 'the same fate as the poor'.

Poverty, the way I understand it, consists not simply in the deprivation of material things, food, shelter, education and so on, but in the absence, or loss of what most people need to live their life fully. Understood in this light, poverty encompasses a multitude of losses: bereavement, physical and mental handicap, illness, depression and plain ordinary loneliness and misery. A multitude of people, therefore, are called to suffer, though for many this suffering will be endured in the secrecy of their own hearts, as they yearn for love or for freedom or simply for a greater fullness of living.

I believe that Good Friday people, like the *Anawim*, are very specially loved by God, for he has called them to walk towards him along a particularly narrow path, the road to Calvary, the same road as his Son. I believe most deeply that they do not walk this path by chance and that they do not walk it in vain. I have no clever answer to the eternal 'Why?' of suffering but I am convinced that whatever its cause and whatever its outcome, it is never without meaning. Just what that meaning is I can only guess: perhaps different people's suffering has different meanings. Some are clearly purified and strengthened by it and go on to do great things for God and his people. Others are quite simply broken, dehumanized and destroyed. Some are ruined before they can even begin: the parcel unwrapped with such eagerness and hope reveals only a pitiful collection of broken shards, wrecked beyond any hope of repair. Such are the children damaged in utero or at birth, or so wounded in childhood that they remain warped and stunted forever.

These are the things that make people 'lose' their faith. How, they say, can there be a loving God, if this goes on? How could God do this to my son? How could he let this happen? Why was the flower of hope that sprang up in China in 1989 crushed so brutally in Tienneman Square? Of what use was the amazing courage of the nameless young man who stood empty-handed in front of the oncoming tanks?

This book does not set out to answer these questions, but to walk the way of the cross alongside Jesus and his companions. This 'way of the cross' is not quite the same as the traditional 'stations of the cross' but starts sometime before, at the point where Jesus 'set his face towards Jerusalem'. This is what I have called the *Kairos* moment, the moment of acceptance or choice, of the call to suffering, and I have tried to show that this is a pivotal event for those whose later distress may make little sense.

The other way in which my journey differs from the 'stations' is that it goes *beyond* the cross, right through to the resurrection. I believe this to be enormously important, for so often terrible suffering is quite overpowering to the onlooker unless it is viewed in the light of the resurrection. I have found this paschal overview enormously helpful in enabling me to work each day with people who are suffering. I do not pretend that it takes the pain away, or the anger or the sense of impotence, but it does make some kind of sense of it all. It's not so much that I believe in pie in the sky, or a happy ending but that I touch the mystery of the risen Christ somehow permeating the suffering, suffusing the darkness.

It's not always so easy, of course. Sometimes everything seems black and sour and there seems no trace of hope or of God. Dan Berrigan captures this sense of the absence of God:

> Why then endure
> why thirst for justice?
> Your kingdom-come
> a mirage which never comes.
>
> I sweat like a beast
> my nightmare is life long
> And where in the world
> are you?
>
> 'And Where in the World are You'
> *Uncommon Prayer*

One gets this sense of the absence of God in some of the descriptions of the German concentration camps. I searched in Elie Wiesel's *Night* for some echo of my own spiritual experience in prison, but found only the devastating, dehumanizing side of things. And yet, in one of his most terrible descriptions, the execution of a child, Wiesel captures the deepest theological reality:

> Where is God? Where is He? someone behind me asked . . . Where is God now? And I heard a voice within me answer him: Where is He? Here He is – He is hanging here on this gallows.

For Elie Wiesel, a deeply religious Jewish boy of fourteen reared on the Talmud and longing to be initiated into the mystical writings of the cabbala, both God and his faith died in Auschwitz.

> Never shall I forget that night, the first night in the camp,

> which has turned my life into one long night, seven times cursed and seven times sealed. Never shall I forget that smoke. Never shall I forget the little faces of the children whose bodies I saw turned into wreaths of smoke beneath a silent blue sky. Never shall I forget those flames which consumed my faith forever. Never shall I forget that nocturnal silence which deprived me, for all eternity, of the desire to live. Never shall I forget those moments which murdered my God and my soul and turned my dreams to dust. Never shall I forget these things, even if I am condemned to live as long as God Himself. Never.

François Mauriac, who met Wiesel, described him as having the look of 'a Lazarus risen from the dead, yet still a prisoner within the grim confines where he had strayed, stumbling among the shameful corpses'. Rich in faith himself, Mauriac could find no words to release the young man from his prison.

> And I, who believe that God is Love, what answer could I give my young questioner, whose dark eyes still held the reflection of that angelic sadness which had appeared one day upon the face of the hanged child? What did I say to him? Did I speak of that other Israeli, his brother, who may have resembled him – the Crucified, whose Cross has conquered the world? Did I affirm that the stumbling block to his faith was the cornerstone of mine, and that the conformity between the Cross and the suffering of men was in my eyes the key to that impenetrable mystery whereon the faith of his childhood had perished? Zion, however, has risen up again from the crematories and the charnel houses. The Jewish nation has been resurrected from among its thousands of dead. It is through them that it lives again. We do not know the worth of one single drop of blood, one single tear. All is grace. If the Eternal is the Eternal, the last word for each one of us belongs to Him. This is what I should have told this Jewish child. But I could only embrace him, weeping.
>
> François Mauriac in the Introduction to
> *Night* by Elie Wiesel

I'm sure Mauriac knew deep in his heart, as I know from my experience of accompanying the suffering, that his tears were worth more than a thousand theological explanations. And yet, as thinking, rational human beings we must always struggle to make sense of the dual realities of our life as Christians: the existence of appalling wickedness and suffering, and our belief in a loving God. Each time I get drawn into this search I find myself caught up in the mystery and paradox of the Scriptures, particularly the Fourth Song of the Servant.

> 'Who could believe what we have heard,
> and to whom has the power of Yahweh been revealed?'
> Like a sapling he grew up in front of us,
> like a root in arid ground.
> Without beauty, without majesty (we saw him),
> no looks to attract our eyes;
> a thing despised and rejected by men,
> a man of sorrows and familiar with suffering,
> a man to make people screen their faces;
> he was despised and we took no account of him.
>
> And yet ours were the sufferings he bore,
> ours the sufferings he carried.
> But we, we thought of him as someone punished,
> struck by God, and brought low.
> Yet he was pierced through for our faults,
> crushed for our sins.
> On him lies a punishment that brings us peace,
> and through his wounds we are healed.[1]

It is this passage, I think, more than any other, that has brought me to where I now stand in my understanding of the mystery of suffering, for I see in the 'man of sorrows' the face not only of Jesus but of all my Good Friday people. There are the people who make us want to screen our faces, to turn away, and yet it is through them that the grace of God flows to water our arid souls. These people are the hollowed bamboo through which the life-giving water flows, the reed pipes on which the musician plays his song.

Do not be surprised, then, if reading this book is hard: there is a terrible agony in watching someone hollowed out with a knife, even if the end result is an instrument on which is played the music of the universe. But remember, too, that these people who walk in darkness are the same people upon whom a light has shone. All the footgear of battle, the sickness and the pain are rolled away and their joy is that of men who rejoice at harvest time, for they, the barren women who bore no children, have become the spouse of him who is the God of the whole earth.

Before we go any further, let me tell you a little about my Good Friday people, for they are woven in and out of narrative rather than appearing in any logical order. They fall, I think, into two broad groups: the victims of violence and those who are physically ill. If those whose lives are caught up in oppression seem larger than life figures, don't be deceived. In some ways, they *are* larger than life, because the martyrs always leave us feeling weak and foolish. But they are real people, men and women like ourselves whose lives happen to be lived out on a very different stage from our own. They are the weak whom God has chosen and made strong, icon figures in whom his power shines through with amazing brightness. All of this group, except one, come from El Salvador, a tiny war-torn country in Central America, although only two of them are native Salvadorans.

The first of these is Archbishop Oscar Romero, the Archbishop of San Salvador who was assassinated in 1980. He is, indeed, a giant figure, a timid rather conservative priest who, by plunging himself into the dark chaotic waters of his ravaged country, was somehow reborn as its defender. (I have developed this image of baptism at some length in the closing chapter for it is crucial to the understanding of how the Church makes sense of suffering and death.) Alongside Archbishop Romero I have introduced another Salvadoran priest who is much less well-known. Father Rutilio Grande. He too was a weak man chosen and made strong in bearing witness and he too was killed for speaking out on behalf of the poor.

There are three other figures from El Salvador, two of whom were personal friends of mine, Maryknoll missionaries from the United States. Both of them chose to work in Salvador in response to a request from the Archbishop and both died in the same year, 1980. Carla Piette, a tall zany artistic redhead, was drowned when the van she was driving overturned in a flash flood. Ita Ford, her close friend and colleague, escaped death, only to be killed by the security forces a few months later. I have written much about these two, not just because they are close to my heart but because the study of the way God worked in and through them is a constant source of wonder to me.

With Ita Ford and two other sisters, Dorothy Kazel and Maura Clarke, there died a young American lay-woman called Jean Donovan. I have learned a good deal about Jean from a carefully researched biography *Salvador Witness* by Anna Carrigan[2] and a documentary film called *Roses in December*. Jean's story is particularly interesting for she is in some ways a very unlikely martyr, being a rather outspoken motorcycle-riding American socialite. Once again I have tried to trace how Jean grew until her knowledge and love of God had been 'pressed by the anguish of life into a single living ferment'.[3]

The last of my victims of violence is the Chilean folk singer Victor Jara, who was tortured and killed shortly after the coup of 1973. Victor is a very earthy figure who has become a hero for thousands of young people throughout the world and he stands as an archetype of the many agnostic men and women who have died like Christ, and for his people while being themselves estranged from Christianity.

My other Good Friday people are perhaps easier to identify with. There is Father Jimmy Doherty, an Irish priest with Multiple Sclerosis, and David, a boy who died with a brain tumour. Then there is Suzi Lovegrove: a very remarkable young Australian woman whose courage in facing death from AIDS was captured on a television film.

The last and most terrible to look upon in this unlikely group on the road to Calvary are the people of Auschwitz, those who were present at the execution of God. They are, indeed, people to make us screen our faces for there can be few regimes in the history of oppression which have deliberately incinerated little children.

As I said, this is not a book for the faint-hearted and, indeed, some of it was very hard to research and to write. There were times when I wondered why on earth I was doing it and where I was going, but quite suddenly I found that I had passed beyond the cross and could see it, as it were, from the other side. It is this part of the journey, more than anything, that has been a joy and a revelation to me, for I have in a very real way discovered the depth of my Christian roots. This particular faith journey has forced me to look deeply not only into the Scriptures but into the liturgy of the Easter Triodion in both the Roman and the Orthodox traditions. I have tried hard to explain what I found on this voyage of discovery, to convey the excitement and joy that accompanied it, the amazing mystery in the story of an Immortal Lover who decides to wed his world, and whose marriage bed is the grave.

Lord we believe,
help thou our unbelief.
We believe in you:
Show us your face.
We believe you love us,
though you test our faith.
In darkness and doubt,
in suffering and despair,
we cling to that faith
with bleeding fingernails.
Lord Our God, we cry to thee:
from the depths of Sheol,
we call your name.
Show us your mercy,
lest we lose hope.
Break down the gates
that hold us captive,
and blind us with the light
of your dazzling darkness.

2

A Man Like Us

His state was divine,
yet he did not cling
to his equality with God,
but emptied himself
to assume the condition of a slave,
and became as men are.

Phil. 2:6f

When I was a child, I thought of God as somewhere out there, in heaven, beyond the stars or at least safely anchored in Church, and I was quite unfamiliar with the Eastern concept of God 'within' me. I could cope with the idea of the Incarnation, because two thousand years seems a very long time ago and Jesus was clearly very special and very different from myself. The familiar portraits of the pale Galilean, however, with his long hair and white robe did nothing to help me identify with the God who became 'as men are' but emasculated him into a fairy-tale character with increasingly little impact upon my life.

It wasn't just a question of an anachronistic portrayal of Jesus in art but I was somehow brought up with such a pious caricature of the man that I never really *met* the real Jesus of the Gospels. Now, in my middle years, I search anew to know not the Father, the unknowable, transcendent God of the mountain (who, in a sense, I 'know' already), but his Son, the Word made Flesh.

Jesus of Nazareth lived two thousand years ago and, along with other men of his time and place, he may well have had long hair and worn a long white nightie. But there is much more to it than that.

If he was truly man, as the evangelists delight in telling

us, then he loved and laughed as we do; he was sometimes tired or hungry, bored, irritated, depressed or just plain fed up. Perhaps, like us, he was unwittingly hurtful, even picked his nose when no one was looking. He had friends, men friends and women too, some close, perhaps very close. Was he celibate? We assume so. Did he yearn sometimes for sexual intimacy? Surely, for he was a normal man, flesh of our flesh.

Why, I wonder, do we shy away from even thinking of Jesus in this way? When, from time to time, film directors have the courage to portray Jesus in modern guise, with normal emotions and sexual fantasies we blush and look away or get hurt and angry and talk of blasphemy. But surely this is nonsense. Why do we *need* a pale sexless softly spoken Jesus with soulful brown eyes any more than we need a sugar-coated, luminous, blue-eyed virgin to be the mother of our God?

A number of years ago I was invited to give a talk on Our Lady to a group of monks and pious laymen. Clearly no one had told them that I was the only child in a Catholic boarding school who had refused to be a 'child of Mary', and that I had a deep antipathy to the Rosary and suchlike devotions. Not to be defeated, however, I accepted and set about rediscovering the Mary of the Gospels. I called my talk 'Our Lady after the Nitromors' (Mary after the Paint Stripper). My technique was simple: wiping out all previous ideas of Mary inculcated during a Catholic childhood I returned to the Gospels to see what was *really* there. I won't go in detail into what I found, but it's an exercise worth doing for there emerges a faint but beautiful outline of a strong woman with whom, surprise surprise, even I could identify. I think it's time, perhaps, that I did the same for Jesus.

I know it's been done before: of course it has, many times, but perhaps each generation needs to apply its own coat of paint stripper and remove the layers so lovingly applied by its forefathers. It's a bit like the stripped pine business: a few years ago my sister Margaret would comb the furniture shops in search of old pine furniture which she then ruthlessly stripped and waxed 'til the beauty of the natural wood was revealed. Now, twenty years later, she still searches for old pine, but now it is for her daughter Emma who is an artist and makes her living by painting furniture. I love Emma's work with its exotic colours and strange mystical animals but I giggle a little to myself when I think that even in Emma's lifetime someone may come along and pour paint stripper over her handiwork and scrape away at the blue-green blisters of paint until the bare wood underneath is revealed. Life was ever thus. Fashions change. Bare cathedrals are embellished with gilt or carvings or marble plaques until the original lines are quite obliterated. I walk around old cathedrals longing to rip out the Victorian memorials and the marble tombs and rediscover the vast sense of emptiness that speaks to me of God more powerfully than a hundred statues. Perhaps that's *it*: what speaks to *me* of God and makes me want to lie pole-axed in adoration on the bare floor may well mean nothing to another person. I think it's like that with the Jesus stories too. There's a terrible grain of truth in the atheist's cynical comment, 'And in the beginning, man created God.' Quite unconsciously, we fashion our ideas of God to suit ourselves, instead of having the courage to lay aside our preconceptions and search for the truth. What if scholarship revealed that Jesus was married? After all, we don't hear a thing about him between the ages of thirteen and thirty. Maybe he married and his wife died – or perhaps he left her at home with the children and went off on his preaching mission. Or, perhaps he was gay. After all he was a *man*, and we know that, for whatever reason, a certain proportion of men and women are gay.

Let me be very clear here: I am not suggesting that Jesus was married nor am I suggesting that he was gay. No. I'm just trying to show that we interpret the gaps in the gospel in a certain way, making assumptions about Jesus that suit us as individuals and as a community of people with very fixed ideas about how things should be. Perhaps it doesn't matter that we do this – or does it? Could it be that by filling in the missing parts of the picture with our own design we are seriously distorting the original? It's as if we have been given an ancient and very beautiful mural and, maddened by the gaps and blurred edges, we have lovingly touched it up until it is as near perfect as we can make it. The question is, of course, have we unwittingly altered the picture beyond all recognition?

The layperson, of course, will say, exasperated, 'But does

it really matter? A picture's only a picture after all.' But the art historian will be white with rage and grief because he knows deep in his guts that it *does* matter, because the truth *always* matters.

The longer I live, the more I, too, know that the truth is somehow enormously important because, in a way that I do not fully understand, God is caught up in it. Jesus' comment that the truth will set you free seems to apply in more and morc areas of life, though as the poster on my noviciate wall reminded me daily, first it may make us miserable!

This 'call' to live the truth (if that's not a pompous way of putting it) has had certain repercussions in my life, which have, in the long run, been enormously freeing. I think it began to take on a conscious shape about five years ago when I embarked upon a period of psychotherapy. As I explored certain areas of my past, particularly childhood events, with the therapist I learned that I could speak the truth about hidden areas of my life without being condemned. Little by little, in the safety of the therapeutic relationship, I learned that not only was I acceptable, even lovable, as a person but that I was really very like other people. Oh how we torture ourselves that we are somehow not worthy, different, not as good as the rest. We think that we are greedy or selfish or sexually not quite right and spend vital emotional energy pretending to be holier or wholer than our neighbour. What a relief it is when we confess the truth of how we really are and learn to our great laughter that we are no worse than our ancestors. The great liberating truth is that we are all, all, vulnerable wounded people and that that is the way God made us.

If this great insight seems a touch banal, forgive me, but like so many other self-evident truths, we don't actually live it! Part of our innate foolishness is that we like to put people into neat categories. We place the Mother Teresas of our world safely on a pedestal where we can admire them but not feel in any way obliged to emulate them. At the other end of the scale are the foreigners, the people with unpronounceable names and an incomprehensible language. And then, right beyond the pole are sinners and the perverts: the muggers, the murderers, the rapists and the child abusers. They are so obviously alien that they must be locked away, for their own safety and for ours. And somewhere in the middle are the sick, the mad, the handicapped, the gays, the transvestites, the drug addicts, the alcoholics and all the other people who we could broadly class as NQOKD (not quite our kind, dear!).

Forgive me: I only write like this because I am a prize categorizer and it took four years in Chile, two months of them in gaol, to convince me that foreigners were real people. Mercifully, my education didn't end when I came out of gaol. For eighteen months I travelled the world as a Human Rights lecturer, speaking my truth before governors and kings, American bishops, a Finnish tribunal and the Swedish parliament. I travelled Scandinavia with a Chilean folk-group, lectured in Spanish to the Norwegians and preached in the cathedral in Stockholm. I wept with exhaustion in more places than I can remember and hurled by Bible in fury and despair at the wall after a three-hour press conference in Copenhagen when I thought I wasn't going to get my lunch! After this great Joan of Arc mission, I took time out and went to live on the edge of a men's monastery, not to rest or lick my wounds but in search of the 'dry martyrdom' of monastic life. Eighteen months of quasi-monastic life and friendship with a number of monks taught me that they too were human and frail and wounded like the rest of us.

Then came the convent and my *real* experience of religious life. After eighteen months of trying too hard to be holy I was asked to leave because I was so miserable. The reasons for my unhappiness have more to do with the system than with any individual sister but as I keep repeating: people are vulnerable and people are flawed and they hurt each other. That's the way life is. That's the way God made people.

So, you see, I know too much about nuns and monks to want to put them on a pedestal and revere them, in the same way that I know too much about doctors and nurses to want to revere them either. Some of them I respect very deeply, some I admire and some I love, but I don't fool myself or them that they are any holier than the next person. It seems to me that people are holy in their different ways, according to their gifts and circumstances. Nowadays, the people I really admire are those who are gentle and selfless with their time and in particular those who are able to accept the more wounded of God's people without question or judgement. My respect is something that I can only give freely, not a tithe that I pay to the church or a tax for the government of the day. If this makes me a touch irreverent with the Church and state then I'm quite ready to explain why.

Now back to Jesus, God made man, Emmanuel, God-with-us. What was he like? We are told again and again that he was a man like us in all things but sin, so perhaps the crucial thing in understanding what he was like is knowing the difference between ordinary human frailty and sin. Let me say right now that sometimes I find the distinction difficult and sometimes, perhaps, the goalposts move. Take being sharp with people, for example. Sometimes at work I'm terribly tired and stressed and, quite unintentionally, I'm very terse with people or downright rude and they are, not unreasonably, hurt! I see that kind of situation as sad and messy but not really sinful, in the way that it would be wrong for me to hurt someone quite deliberately for fun or because I dislike them. One can extend this principle into all sorts of areas such as theft or sexuality. What is clearly wrong for an adult with normal self-control can be barely culpable in someone whose age, intellect or social situation render them infinitely more vulnerable. As I said, the goalposts move and this is one reason that priests and pastors need to learn psychology so that they can understand what drives people to behave in the way they do.

And what about Jesus? Was he always sweet-tempered? It seems no, for he vented a good deal of holy anger on the unfortunate merchants in the temple. What, I wonder, were his other weaknesses, for surely he must have had them? Perhaps it doesn't really matter what they are so long as we realize that, being human, he must have had them.

This leads me to a particular time in Jesus' life and to certain specific aspects of his humanity: his passion and death. In the chapters that follow I'd like to do precisely what I have complained that Christians have been doing for the past two thousand years: *speculate* on what Jesus was like as he faced his impending death. I believe it is important to do this not just because Jesus died for us two thousand years ago but because there are countless other men and women who also die cruel and painful deaths for their fellows. I find it impossible to believe that these deaths are not somehow linked – as T. S. Eliot puts it:

> The Son of Man is not crucified once for always.
> The blood of martyrs is not shed once for always
> But the Son of Man is crucified always
> And there shall be martyrs and saints.
>
> from '*Choruses from "The Rock"*'

I believe that we have much to learn about Jesus' passion from the suffering of those more accessible to us and that it is profoundly unhealthy to concentrate upon Jesus suffering while ignoring the cruelty and torture which are endemic in our world.

I have never been a great devotee of the Stations of the Cross, that traditional Catholic devotion which meditates upon the different stages of Jesus' journey towards Calvary. Somehow I've never been able to think myself into the shadows of Pilate's court or hear the swish of the cords as he is scourged; perhaps it's because I have little taste or facility for imaginative prayer. Since my time in Chile, however, things are somehow different: in some ways much worse. Now that I have experienced, in my own flesh, what it is like to be powerless and brutalized I cannot reflect upon the passion without such a reawakening of personal memories that I feel physically sick.

So why do I write now? Perhaps it's important for all of us, from time to time, to share as deeply as we are able in the pain of our fellows. It is part of the quest for truth and it makes us more available to comfort those who have suffered more than men and women *should* be asked to bear. In London, Toronto, Copenhagen and elsewhere there are doctors, and other health workers, who listen, day after day, to the sad tales of torture, depression and despair of ex-prisoners of conscience and who, in exposing themselves to another's pain, are part of the healing process. In the same way hospice workers expose themselves to the terrible desolation of those dying of cancer. Pain is part of the human condition and sharing that pain is a deeply human task.

Let me, then, introduce you to my Good Friday people, and challenge you to walk with them as far as you dare. In sharing their pain, humiliation and despair you will be sharing perhaps more deeply than ever before in the Jesus story, for did he not himself say, 'whatever you do to the least of my brethren, you do it indeed unto me'?

Lord Jesus Christ, Son of the Living God,
show us your face.
We long to know you, in spirit and in truth,
for you are the Way to freedom.
Teach us to love your people,
as you and the Father love them,
to be slow to anger and rich in mercy.
Help us to understand ourselves,
to cherish your life within us
that we may become as you were,
a place of refuge for the lonely, the wounded and the sinner.

3

Called to Powerlessness

Do not be afraid, for I have redeemed you,
I have called you by your name, you are mine.
Isa. 43:1

One day, we're told, Jesus said to his disciples, 'If anyone wants to be a follower of mine, let him renounce himself daily and take up his cross daily and follow me. For anyone who wants to save his life will lose it, but anyone who loses his life for my sake, that man will save it.'[1]

Of all the uncomfortable, upsetting gospel texts, this must surely be amongst the most unnerving. What on earth, I wonder, did the disciples make of it, coming as it did immediately after the first time that Jesus broke it to them that his ministry would inevitably end in his death? And when, I wonder, did it first dawn on Jesus that he was running head long into trouble?

We know tantalizingly little of Jesus' sense of call. Clearly something hapened to him as a youth when he found himself so at home among the learned men in the temple.[2] We see a parallel in those young men and women who somehow know from childhood that they are marked out for service. And what of the hidden years at Nazareth? Did Jesus really spend the next eighteen years as a carpenter, and if he did what happened to his sense of call? Did it lie dormant, forgotten all those years, only to surface again in his thirties? Or was it a steadily growing conviction that he had to go out and preach in God's name? Did he perhaps resist the call? If he did he wouldn't be the first or the last. As I suggested before, perhaps he was married, as most men of his age and social situation would have been. The idea seems preposterous, doesn't it: almost a blasphemy. But why? Why should it matter to us that Jesus might have been married, even had children? Does it threaten our concept of a celibate priesthood perhaps, undermine the foundations of our carefully constructed house of cards? True, there is no mention of a wife: but then the only reference to the fact that any of the disciples had a wife is to Simon's mother-in-law. So what about the disciples?

One presumes they were married and that their wives were at home looking after the children. Did Jesus call his disciples permanently away from their families, I wonder? In the famous call passage in Luke 18:18ff which has haunted me for so many years, Jesus tells the rich young man, 'There is still one thing that you lack. Sell all that you own and distribute the money to the poor, and you will have treasure in heaven; then come, follow me.'

The young man, we are told, went away sad, for he was very rich and Jesus sighed and commented how hard it was for the rich to abandon their possessions and enter the Kingdom. Peter, who clearly had left a good deal more behind than a leaking boat and his nets, demanded to know what would be their reward. Jesus' answer was very clear, 'I tell you solemnly, there is no one who has left house, wife, brothers, parents or children for the sake of the kingdom of God who will not be given repayment many times over in the present time and in the world to come, eternal life'. This is a very familiar and comforting passage to those who enter religious life and is usually taken to refer to those who have abandoned their parents and siblings and the *opportunity* of marriage, for the sake of the Kingdom. I'm not at all sure, however, that that's what Jesus meant here because he doesn't say leave 'the possibility of getting married' but speaks quite clearly of those who have 'left wife'. One wonders a little how the wives felt when their men went off after this entrancing pied piper. Perhaps they weren't quite so enthusiastic, who knows?

And what of Jesus himself? Did he know right from the beginning that his message would land him in trouble? After all, it seems he began his ministry soon after John the Baptist was imprisoned. It wasn't until much later, however, that he spoke so clearly of the risks to his disciples: 'Beware of men: they will hand you over to sanhedrins and scourge you in their synagogues. You will be dragged before governors and kings for my sake, to bear witness before them and the pagans.'[3]

This call to powerlessness for the sake of the gospel has become a familiar characteristic of the Christian vocation right up to our own day. It is seen most clearly, of course, in the call of the missionary, in the life of people like Ita Ford or Jean Donovan who by their very 'fiat' accept the possibility of working in troubled lands.

Jean's call began in her teens when she was studying in Cork on a high school exchange programme and became friends with the chaplain, ex-missionary Father Michael Crowley.

'The one experience he related to me the most was concerning his time as a missionary in Peru . . . he helped me explain the calling I was feeling.' This sense of calling was to recur and mature over the years until Jean returned briefly to Ireland and turned up unannounced on Michael Crowley's doorstep.

> Her manner was flip, almost defiant. 'Don't laugh too loud, Mike,' she said, 'I've come to talk to you because I think I have to change my life'. This was no impulse visit: she knew quite well what she was doing when she came to Europe that time, when she was tossing over the idea of becoming a missionary; she was basically saying – life as I live it isn't fulfilling me deep down.[4]

Perhaps that's the magic and the essence of call: the yearning for God deep in our guts that makes total sense of the psalmist's words: 'Your love is better than life itself.'[5] Slowly, Jean's call clarified. Her conversations led to increasing involvement in social justice and community issues in her home town of Cleveland until, one day, she heard of the Cleveland Diocese Mission to El Salvador. That was it. There was no turning back. How well I know that curious phenomenon of certainty after a prolonged and apparently fruitless period of searching. One thrashes about taking endless counsel and then, suddenly, things fall into place, one's previously fluid resolve solidifies, and one is away. But Salvador, 'Why Salvador?' Jean's friends asked her. Her brother Michael, knowing only too clearly the risks of that war-torn country, did his best to dissuade her. 'I don't think,' he says, 'I could have tried harder.' Jean did listen. 'She was very stubborn and determined in most things. On any other subject she would always argue vociferously. But this was totally different. With regard to El Salvador she'd be very still, very quiet. She'd just listen to what everybody had to say – she never really got argumentative about it at all.'[6] Among her closest friends Rita and Mary, Jean puzzled over what was happening to her: '"What does it mean to say: this is something I have to do; this is something that I believe God wants me to do. And why? Why me?" Jean would ask, "Why do I want to do this? Why don't you or Rita want to go to Salvador? Why is this something that I have to do?"'[7]

There is something very dramatic and pure about the missionary call but I am quite clear that it is not only the missionaries who are called to powerlessness. There's a very real sense in which we are all, sooner or later, required to let go of the strings with which we manipulate our lives and be led, as Jesus put it, 'where we would rather not go'. For some, however, this call to let go comes much earlier than they expect and is therefore especially bitter.

David was only eighteen when he began to suspect that something was wrong. His mother took him to see the doctor about the peculiar feelings in his legs but they were told it was because David was anxious about his exams and the feelings were best ignored. Mary, his mother, was to learn the meaning of impotence as her son's condition worsened and the doctor insisted it was psychosomatic. Eventually, in a fury, she went to the doctor's surgery and told him she wasn't going to move until David was seen by a specialist. Even before the CAT scan first revealed the tumour in David's brain Mary knew that her life was changed forever.

How are we to understand those 'acts of God' that draw people to walk along the Calvary road? Does God actively will that David gets a brain tumour, or is it just his 'passive' or 'permissive' will allowing the forces of evil to triumph? I have little taste for the theological niceties about causation of evil: I know only that Mary and David walk the same road as Jesus, as Jean Donovan and as the students in Tienneman Square. They are somehow singled out to share in a very special way in the passion and are thereby caught up in the strange drama of redemptive suffering.

David's and Jean Donovan's are the acceptable face of pain: the innocent victims of fate or of a cruel regime. But what of Suzi, who some people would see as getting no more than she deserved, catching the HIV virus in a fleeting illicit sexual encounter in New York? I choose Suzi deliberately for she is neither gay nor haemophiliac and there are few who could not look at her and say, 'There but for the grace of God go I'. The world is not divided into the good and the bad, the chaste and the profligate, the straight and the gay, for we are all sinners, all wounded and I suspect we would none of us feel qualified to cast the first stone. So I see Suzi alongside Jesus on that cruel road, close to him as Mary Magdalen was close, bearing the cross of all the women over the centuries who have loved too much but are surely forgiven more than those who buried their love like a talent in the ground for fear that it be stolen.

There they walk together, my Good Friday people, at the beginning of their journey. They have set out in response to a call, and march to a different drummer, though as yet they may be barely aware that the music has changed. Just why they are called we do not know except that they are somehow caught up in the destiny of an itinerant preacher, whether they like it or not. Some of them will protest loudly along the way, like the prophet Jeremiah:

> You have seduced me, Lord, and I have let myself be seduced.
> You have overpowered me: you were the stronger.[8]

And others will go quietly, growing into their vocation like Oscar Romero, the conservative Bishop of San Salvador who set out to defeat his rebel priests but ended up their champion.

Oscar Arnulfo Romero was named Archbishop of San Salvador on 28 February 1977. He was a quiet man, an introvert who believed that prayer and personal conversion were what mattered and who liked to keep his distance from the more revolutionary members of his flock. Little by little, however, he found himself drawn into the struggle of his people until he could declare in public,

> I am a shepherd who, with his people, has begun to learn a beautiful and difficult truth: our Christian faith requires that we submerge ourselves in this world.
>
> The world that the Church must serve is the world of the poor, and the poor are the ones who decide what it means for the Church to really live in the world.[9]

It was the poor who showed the Archbishop what they required of their Church: not just the catechism and the sacraments but something much harder: to speak out against injustice, to be the voice of a people who had no voice. So that is what he did: week by week and month by month his sermons were broadcast to the nation and he denounced the killings endemic among his people. In 1980 he received the Nobel Prize for Peace and at the ceremony in Louvain he declared:

> The Church has committed itself to the world of the poor . . . The words of the prophet of Israel still hold true for us: there are those who would sell a just man for money, and a poor man for a pair of sandals. There are those who fill their houses with violence, fill their houses with what they have stolen. There are those who crush the poor . . . while lying on beds of the most exquisite marble. There are those who take over house after house, field after field, until they own the whole territory and they are the only ones in it.
>
> It is the poor who force us to understand what is really taking place . . . The persecution of the Church is a result of defending the poor. Our persecution is nothing more nor less than sharing in the destiny of the poor.
>
> The poor are the body of Christ today. Through them he lives on in history.[10]

'The poor are the body of Christ today': how clearly he sees it, this Archbishop who has learned to submerge his Church in the world. His concerns are not for rubrics nor the ordination of women or gays but for the care of his people. Again and again I am struck by the clarity of vision of the Church under persecution. It's almost as if when times are good we lose sight of the gospel message and get caught up in ecclesiastical politics and liturgical minutiae.

We squabble like the Pharisees of old about tassles and phylacteries, titles and precedence, forgetting that the man we follow washed his disciples' feet and told them that they should be known not by their purple shirts or pectoral crosses but by their love for one another.

Ironically it is often the non-believers who seem closest to following Jesus' example. Victor Jara, another of my Good Friday people, is one such man. Victor was a Chilean singer, a man of the people who like Romero found himself called to be a voice for the poor. Disillusioned by a Church that offered nothing but promises of heaven to the oppressed peasants he abandoned his studies for the priesthood and put his 'honest guitar' to work.

Victor was in the vanguard of Allende's new government in the way that artists so often are, using his voice to speak out for the hungry, barefoot children of Chile and their desperate parents. Like Jesus, he too was a charismatic figure, drawing the crowds to his concerts as he journeyed from village to village, spreading the good news that liberation was at hand. Is it blasphemous, I wonder, to draw such parallels? Should I be speaking of a Marxist folk-singer in the same breath as Jesus, Son of God? The answer is surely yes, for did not Victor Jara embark upon his road to Calvary in response to a call to serve the poor? I have lived too close to Chilean revolutionaries not to know that their love is more selfless than many of those who condemn them, sight unseen and case unheard.

So there go they together along the road, priests and people, nuns and revolutionaries, archbishops and folk-singers, schoolboys and fallen women. And as they walk they will each, in their own good time, arrive at their Kairos moment, the point of choice, of decision, of a stiffening of the sinews because danger is in the air and there is no turning back.

Lord of the Universe, maker of all:
tune our ears to hear your voice.
Speak to our hearts, we beg.
We dare you, Lord, to bid us 'Come',
to walk to you across the water.
But if you do call,

give us courage,
for we are very scared
of getting out of the boat.

4

Towards Jerusalem

Now as the time drew near for him to be taken up to heaven, he resolutely took the road for Jerusalem.
Luke 9:51

These opening lines of Luke's 'great intercalation' (Luke 9:51–18:14) set the scene for the run-up to Jesus' passion. Drawing from ancient material known as the 'Supplementary Collection' (not available to Mark) he gives us a vivid picture of Jesus' outspoken teaching on justice and the increasing hostility of the Jewish elders. Rereading this section immediately after seeing a film on the life of Archbishop Oscar Romero I am fascinated by the similarity between the two men. The film drew my attention to certain aspects of Archbishop Romero's life which I had not gathered at first reading of Father Erdozain's biography, namely, his increasingly open conflict with the ruling classes in San Salvador. I had forgotten what I had learned during my time in Chile, how great is the contrast in Latin America between the aristocracy and the peasants. It is not simply a question of money and lifestyle but of stature and countenance, for the members of the oligarchies tend to be descendants of the wealthy Spanish aristocracy whilst the peasants are often mestizo, part Indian. The former are often tall and fair, of aquiline countenance while the peasants are much shorter, darker with clear evidence of their Indian roots. In his biography of Romero, Father Erdozain, a close companion of the Archbishop speaks of 'chronological' time and 'Kairotic' time – time beyond measure, the moment of encounter, the opportune time. For Romero, the Kairos, the moment of the total merging of his own destiny with that of his people was the day the first of his priests was murdered for speaking out on behalf of the poor.

Father Rutilio Grande, assassinated on 12 March 1977, is yet another of El Salvador's Good Friday people.

Born in 1927, in the village of El Paisnal, he lost his mother at the age of four. While still a child he met and became friends with Monsignor Luis Chavez, who was destined to precede Oscar Romero as Archbishop of San Salvador. Determined from the age of twelve that he wanted to be a priest, he entered the diocesan minor seminary at the age of thirteen and at seventeen embarked upon his life as a Jesuit.

His early years in the Society seem to have been extremely difficult for he was plagued by a driven and anxious temperament: 'he was constantly tense, depressed, anxious over the quality of his work, his prayer, his dealings with others.'[1] His studies were interrupted because of his health and he was sent to teach in a Jesuit school in Panama and while there was briefly hospitalized because of 'yet another nervous crisis'.[2] In June 1959 he suffered further severe anxiety and scruples about his forthcoming ordination to the priesthood, but was persuaded to go ahead. He remained depressed and fragile after his ordination and returned from Spain to El Salvador to teach in the seminary. After two much happier years he returned rather fearfully to Spain to spend his tertian year. Of this year O'Malley writes, 'His fears proved to have been justified. All the old devils which had been shunted aside during the bustle of active work began to emerge once again from the dark back rooms of his mind.' The following year, however, things were to change for this fragile, neurotic man for he was sent to study at Lumen Vitae, the International Catechetics Institute in Brussels. It was here that his healing was to take place, for he found himself in the much happier atmosphere of a post Vatican II situation. ' . . . The Church's conversion became Rutilio Grande's conversion. Slowly, ever so slowly, he began to see that he was not called to be a perfect plaster Saint unceasingly rapt in adoration; he was called to be a pastor, an outcast and imperfect Samaritan helping his fellow outcasts who lay battered along his road.'[3]

In 1964, Rutilio returned to El Salvador, a much happier and freer man after having resolved during his retreat, 'I promise never to be a perfectionist again. I will learn to swim by swimming. I put all my trust in Jesus; he is the only thing that remains.'[4]

I have laboured a little to sketch this early portrait of the anxious and scrupulous Rutilio because it is in such incredible contrast with the later man, whose courage and single-minded behaviour was to lead inexorably to his murder. In 1965 he returned once more to the seminary in San Salvador as a professor of pastoral theology and director of the social action projects of the seminarians where he was to have a crucial role in formation of El Salvador's future priests and, therefore, in moulding its Church.

Rutilio brought to the training of his young priests the ideals of Vatican II which had so changed his own life in Belgium. Instead of giving his students theses to memorize as was the tradition, he sent them to meet their future parishioners, to live and work in the suburbs and shanty towns.

It is difficult to convey to someone unfamiliar with the reality of life in Latin America the impact of such an experience on young, middle-class students. It was no coincidence that the majority of the women that I met in my own time in prison in Santiago were youngsters from comfortable homes whose professional training had brought them into intimate contact with the lives of the poor. I remember, too, my own feelings as I worked in a peripheral children's hospital and then in a shanty town clinic as the reality of the life of the people hit me. However much one may know about poverty and oppression at an intellectual level, *meeting* the poor themselves is something quite other. I recall to this day the sense of bewilderment and outrage that I experienced as I interviewed woman after woman whose children were dying of diarrhoea or malnutrition and learned that they had already lost one, two or three children in the same way. I remember too the sight of a young couple walking slowly away from the hospital bearing only the shawl of their baby who had just died.

How much greater must have been the impact on these young Salvadorans not just to care for these people but to live amongst them, sharing their appalling conditions, their hopes and their despair. They returned after these periods of pastoral experience to reflect upon what they had seen and heard and to try to make sense of it in the light of the gospel. How they must have pored over the parable of the good

Samaritan with its call to bind up the wounds of the stranger and Jesus' furious discourse against the rich and hypocritical: 'Woe to you, Pharisees, for you tithe mint and rue and every herb, and neglect justice and love of God! These you should have done without neglecting the others. Woe, you Pharisees! For you love the best seat in the synagogue and salutations in the market place.'[5]

It is hard for us first world people to appreciate the dynamite quality of this familiar New Testament text. We hear something about tithes on mint and rue and think 'how quaint', and miss the accusation of justice ignored. But in the Third World the injustice is so much more obvious that the words have a terrible immediacy. Let me return for a moment to Archbishop Romero's Nobel Prize acceptance speech:

> The words of the prophets of Israel still hold true for us: there are those who would sell a just man for money and a poor man for a pair of sandals. There are those who fill their houses with violence, fill their houses with what they have stolen. There are those who crush the poor . . . while lying on beds of the most exquisite marble.

The seminarians' exposure to the reality of poverty and oppression of their fellow countrymen and women was to have a lasting effect. For many of them who came from wealthy families their vision of the priesthood was turned quite upside-down by this professor who had started life as a peasant. They lost forever the idea that being a parish priest was a simple matter of saying mass, baptizing and burying, and taking tea with the ladies of the parish. It was here, too, that they rediscovered the Old Testament concept of God as the liberator of his oppressed people.

In 1970, after five years of teaching in the seminary, Rutilio was asked by his mentor, the Archbishop, to preach the homily in the cathedral on the national feast of the Transfiguration. For better or for worse, he spoke his truth – a call to personal and social transfiguration of both rich and poor. 'Because we are all of us both baptized and citizens, the church and the government must collaborate efficaciously, audaciously, urgently to work out just, honest, decent laws to transfigure the Salvadoran people. Only then can we call Cristo Salvador Transfigurado our patron.'

This fiery sermon, delivered in the presence of the President and ecclesiastical dignitaries as well as the ordinary people, destroyed for ever Rutilio's prospects of being the next rector of the seminary and brought about a change in direction which was to have even more far-reaching consequences.

Rutilio left the seminary and after a year as principal of a wealthy boys' school took a year out to do a course at the Latin American Pastoral Institute in Equador. It was there that he found the time to reflect and formulate plans for his future ministry: the formation of a pastoral team to work in a rural or a slum area to begin the process of what in Latin America is known as concientization: the raising of awareness among the poor of their dignity and rights as human beings and as children of God.

The crucial role of the Latin American Church's policy of concientization, following upon its Option for the Poor at the Conference of Medellin, cannot be overestimated. In order to appreciate its importance we must understand certain things.

First, the Church had for centuries aligned itself with the rich landowners rather than the poor and had taught a vision of God which encouraged the poor to accept their lot as divinely ordained and therefore not to be questioned i.e.

> The rich man in his castle,
> The poor man at his gate,
> God made them, high or lowly,
> And ordered their estate.
>
> Cecil Frances Alexander
> *All Things Bright and Beautiful*

The second is that the Second Vatican Council and the Conference at Medellin rediscovered the practical implication of Jesus' mission to bring 'good news to the poor and freedom to captives'. By taking the gospel seriously they inevitably set about destabilizing a status-quo which had been accepted for hundreds of years in which a small minority of wealthy people lived in luxury *at the expense of* the majority of the poor.

This change in pastoral policy brought about by a renewed understanding of the gospel lies at the heart of the political conflict in Latin America. It is not a simple issue of priests and nuns naughtily becoming involved in politics, but of the Church in her option for the poor and preaching of the gospel to them *inevitably* taking part in the process of awakening a sleeping giant. Living among the peasants, sharing their life and understanding their needs, they would then help them to realize not only what their life *was* like but what it could and should be like. Lastly, their overtly spiritual ministry was to help them to see their lives in relation to the liberating message of the gospel.

In keeping with the movement within the Church, Rutilio deliberately set out to awaken his people. This was not one trouble-making priest but an honest professor of theology following the recommendations of the bishops at the Conference of Medellin: 'The Church must encourage and favour the efforts of the people to create and develop their grass roots organizations in order to restore and consolidate their rights and their search for true justice.'

In September 1972, Father Rutilio Grande and his team came to work in the town of Aguilares, to bring the light of the gospel to a people who, until now, had walked in darkness.

Perhaps I should enlarge a little on my reference here to the prophet Isaiah.

> The people that walked in darkness
> has seen a great light;
> on those who live in a land of deep shadow
> a light has shone.[6]

The poor of Latin America are truly a people who have walked in darkness for centuries for not only is their understanding of God and his purposes deeply flawed but the poverty of their life is such that they are trapped by their lack of education, decent housing, health care and work in a vicious circle which has been described as institutionalized violence. Dom Helder Camara, the fiery Archbishop of Brazil's North East, speaks of the situation of the poor as being like a stagnant pool. No shots may be fired, no stones thrown, but babies die of malnutrition and diarrhoea and children grow up barefoot and illiterate less than five miles from the homes of those who enjoy a university education and all the comforts of the First World.

When Karl Marx spoke of Religion as the 'opium of the people' he was not without reason, for the poor's understanding of God is frequently bound up with primitive superstition and they see the Christian God not as their liberator nor as their loving father but rather a grander and more implacable figure than their 'patron', the landowner upon whose dry earth they hold an uncertain and expensive tenancy. It is in perpetuating and fostering this image of God that the Church has colluded with the rich in order to maintain the false and stinking peace of a status quo in which ten per cent of the inhabitants of a country own ninety per cent of its resources while the rest eke out a subhuman existence until they die before their time.

This is the situation that Rutilio and his teams of Jesuit priests set out to change: to bring to the people a vision of a different God: a God who loves his people with an everlasting love, a Jesus who at the outset of his public ministry chose the text:

> He has sent me to bring good news to the poor,
> freedom to captives,
> to bind up hearts that are broken and to set the
> downtrodden free.[7]

For the next five years Rutilio and his team worked among the people of Aguilares and its surrounding countryside. Their technique was simple and reminiscent of the disciples' mission of evangelization. They went in twos to the villages and lived amongst the people for two weeks at a time, getting to know them, gaining their trust, sharing their lives and learning about their hopes and their despair. Each night they would hold a meeting and explain the Scriptures to the people, encouraging them to discuss and reflect upon just what relevance the Gospels might have upon their lives.

It is not easy for those who have been brought up in a 'Christian civilization', to understand the raw power of the Gospels for those who hunger for justice. Year after year I listen to Isaiah's prophecies read at carol services in our great English cathedrals and grieve that these words have been somehow emasculated, trapped like a fly in the honey of a beautiful liturgy. Ernesto Cardenal, the priest poet from Nicaragua, gives us a glimpse of how the poor, hungry for the message of freedom locked in the Gospels, tear it apart with their bare hands until the sweet juice runs free: listen to

Cardenal facilitating a discussion on Matthew 11, the story in which Jesus sends a coded message to John the Baptist languishing in prison, in response to his request to know if Jesus was the Messiah.

> CARDENAL: Jesus didn't clearly say he was the Messiah, no doubt because it was dangerous to say so. He never said it clearly until they were condemning him to death in the Sanhedrin. What he did here was to say it indirectly to John in such a way that John could understand it: quoting the prophecies of Isaiah, that when the Messiah came, the blind were going to see, the deaf were going to hear, the lame would leap like deer, the dead would come to life again, the poor would learn the good news of their freedom.

> ALEJO'S MOTHER: The poor don't have any freedom, not even freedom to think, and then they can't think about the oppressed situation they're in, and they don't even know they're oppressed, and that message is for them . . . I can't explain it well . . . that message of freedom . . . The poorest of us feel humiliated in a situation where we can't even think about freedom or reach it. And that's why Jesus brings us the good news about a change: that all of us poor people in the country are going to have freedom.[8]

As the two weeks of the Jesuits' 'mission' drew to an end, the people elected men and women as leaders or 'Delegates of the Word', who would continue to lead these Scripture discussions after the priests had left. Thus were formed the grass roots or 'base' communities which were to be the seeds of change, or the small fires of hope which would set alight the tinder box of a parched and despairing continent. It was not that the priests preached revolution but that they showed the people how to discover for themselves that, contrary to what they had been taught for centuries, resignation to their misery was not God's will for them. As Rutilio delighted in telling them: 'God is not somewhere up in the clouds lying in a hammock. God is here with us, building up a Kingdom here on earth.'[9]

Inevitably, the people, once organized to reflect upon the gospel and their lives, used that organization to struggle to change their situation. Little by little they gained the courage to confront the landowners, requesting, then demanding, a living wage and just rents for the infertile land on which they lived. Rutilio Grande saw clearly where the distinction lay between his role as pastor and that of political organizer and he took care not to be used by the emergent political groups. He wrote:

> The ambiguity of the priesthood! Some want him to be a kind of non temporal abstraction. Others want him to be an agitator. He can be neither one nor the other. There is a difference in charisms in the Body of Christ. The priest is the animator of the community toward eternal values, but at the same time toward historical values. It is the members of the community who must now take the eternal values and make them practical with concrete projects and programmes.[10]

However clear the distinction in Rutilio's mind, however, the landowners and those in authority saw things differently and Rutilio began to realize that if he continued in his work his life would perhaps run the samc course as his Master's. By July 1975 he was publicly accused of subversion by the conservative 'Religious Preservation Front' – while at the same time he was condemned by some of his more radical parishioners for lack of commitment to their cause.

As the February 1977 elections approached, the repression against church personnel increased and Rutilio arranged for people to inform the Jesuit provincial should he be arrested. On 13 February Rutilio preached at a gathering of the people as mass was celebrated in the Plaza of the town of Apopa. He used the Genesis story of Cain and Abel to illustrate the way Salvador was divided, brother against brother. His words were fiery and it has been said that it was perhaps this sermon that sealed his death warrant:

> The enslaved masses of our people, those by the side of our road, live in a feudal system six centuries old. They own neither their land nor their own lives. They have to climb up into the trees, and even the trees don't belong to them. Mouths are full of the word 'Democracy', but let us not fool ourselves. There is no democracy when the power of the people is the power of a wealthy minority, not of the

people. You are the Cains, and you crucify the Lord in the person of Manuel, of Luis, of Chavela, of the humble campesino.

There are those in our brotherhood who would prefer a buried Christ, a dummy to carry through the streets in processions, a Christ with a muzzle in his mouth, a Christ made to the specifications of our whims and according to our own petty interests. They do not want a God who will question us and trouble our consciences, a God who cries out: 'Cain! What have you done to your brother Abel?'[11]

In his heartfelt, 'It is dangerous to be a Christian in our world, where the very preaching of the gospel is subversive and where priests are exiled for preaching it!' Rutilio spoke of the new conditions for discipleship under which he and his colleagues now lived. The situation, however, was destined to become worse for the new and fraudulently elected president had promised to rid El Salvador of its turbulent priests, promising that, within three months of his election, there would not be a single Jesuit left in the country. He seemed intent upon fulfilling his pledge, for the day after his election, the first priest, Father Raphael Bahrahona, was kidnapped by the police and tortured.

It was following this violent turn of events that on 22 February Archbishop Chavez, now seventy-five, quietly handed over the reins to Salvador's new Archbishop elect, Oscar Arnulfo Romero.

Just six days later came an event which was to shake Bishop Romero to the core, for at midnight of 28 February, the National Guard opened fire upon a crowd of ten thousand people, gathered in San Salvador's Plaza Libertad to protest against the recent, fraudulent elections. Terrified, the people rushed to take sanctuary in the church of El Rosario but many were killed as the guards shot indiscriminately into the crowd.

The following day the Archbishop met with a group of his priests, many of whom were worried that this man, who was regarded a conservative, would not support them in their struggle. Instead of condemning them for their involvement in politics, however, the Archbishop told them to go home to take care of their people, opening their homes to those who were in danger, hiding them from the police if need arose.

The beginning of the Archbishop's conversion had begun! On 5 March he completed his first pastoral letter to the archdiocese, 'enumerating in terse straightforward language the repressions, killings, tortures, disappearances, campaigns by landowners against the church and Archbishop Chavez, and the deportation of priests without consulting the hierarchy.' The letter stated that even at the risk of being misunderstood the Church has to raise its voice and expose sin wherever it is, 'in the Pharisees, priests, the wealthy, in Herod or Pilate. All are called by God, rich and poor, but the Church must take its stand for the dispossessed.'[12]

Just seven days after that, on Saturday 12 March, 1977, Father Rutilio Grande set out in his jeep with the pastoral letter in his pocket to preach at the evening mass in the village of El Paisnal where he had been born. With him travelled two friends, an old man and a boy, also called Rutilio. Somewhere along the way they gave a lift to three little children and it was these three who were the only witnesses to the bullets which killed Rutilio and his two companions as they drove through the fields to say the vigil mass of the Sabbath.

What did the Archbishop feel when he learned of Rutilio's death? We are not told, only that he went at once to Aguilares where the three bodies had been taken and presided at a mass for those who had died. Jon Sobrino, the Jesuit theologian who was present that night, writes powerfully of the impact of Rutilio's murder upon the Archbishop:

> after mass, Archbishop Romero asked us priests and sisters to remain in the church . . . we held a planning session right there and then in the late hours of the night . . . Archbishop Romero was visibly agitated. He seemed to be labouring under the responsibility of having to do something and not knowing exactly what to do. After all, the problem facing him was unheard of. And the question he asked us was elementary. What should we, and could we, do, as Church, about Rutilio's murder?
>
> I shall never forget how totally sincere he was in asking us to help him – persons whom a few weeks ago he had regarded as suspect, as Marxist. I felt a great tenderness

for that humble bishop, who was asking us, practically begging us, to help him bear the burden that heaven had imposed on him, a far heavier burden than his shoulders, or anyone else's, could have borne alone.

Sobrino clearly feels that this was a Kairos moment for the Archbishop:

> I also felt . . . that something very profound was transpiring deep within Archbishop Romero . . . I think he was forming the high resolve to react in whatever way God might ask: he was making an authentic option for the poor, who had been represented, a scant hour before, by hundreds of campesinos gathered about three corpses, helpless in the face of the repression they had already suffered and knowing full well there was more to come . . . I believe he must have felt that those campesinos had made an option for him – that they were asking for him to defend them. And his response was to make an option for the campesinos – to be converted and transformed into their defender, to become the voice of the voiceless. I believe that Archbishop Romero's definitive conversion began that night.[13]

And so, it seems, that night, a gentle and conservative Archbishop accepted the mantle of his dead son, and turned his face resolutely towards Jerusalem where, so it is written, a shepherd must lay down his life for his people.

Master of all, great and small,
we thank you for your people.
We praise you for the courage
of apostles and martyrs
for those who shine like beacons
in dark and troubled lands.
Seize our hearts, we beg,
and set fire to them,
that we too may cast your light
upon the road to Jerusalem.

5

We Without a Future

We, without a future,
Safe, defined, delivered
Now salute you God,
Knowing that nothing is safe,
Secure, inviolable here.
Except you,
And even that eludes our minds at times.

Anna McKenzie

There is a space, a chronological lapse of time, which is also a spiritual space, between the Kairos moment of choice or knowing and the beginning of the final journey towards death. It is a desert, a bleak, comfortless land in which few birds sing, but it has oases, green patches with tinkling wells where the water is sweet, where bright flowers grow. Here, in these oases, there is the sound of good talk, of friends at play and, from time to time, the ring of laughter under the stars.

This is the land my people enter when they know that the cancer with which they have fought so long has the upper hand and, short of a miracle, they must surely die. I know this land, though not as they do, from firsthand experience; I have not felt in my bones the chill of the desert wind or wept alone in the night in terror at the unknown but I have shared for a time the grief of those who *have* and even that is too close for comfort. Perhaps, in hindsight, I *have* entered that desert myself for one night, long ago I faced the possibility of my own death, not as a pious retreat exercise but in solitary confinement in a Chilean gaol. How well I remember – and long to forget – that night of now done darkness as I digested the reality of what the judge had said to me: that it was by no means certain that I would be expelled and that I would be tried 'according to Chilean law' for a crime which I had not committed.

Mercifully for me, my sojourn in the desert was brief though even so, it was long enough to leave me scarred. For the people with whom I now work, however, there is no consul to negotiate with the powers of death and no war of giants in which the prisoner's release is more expedient that her execution:

> We did not want it easy God,
> But we did not contemplate
> That it would be quite this hard,
> This long, this lonely.
> So, if we are to be turned inside out,
> And upside down,
> With even our pockets shaken
> Just to check what's rattling
> And left behind,
> We pray that you will keep faith with us,
> And we with you,
> Holding our hands as we weep,
> Giving us strength to continue,
> And showing us beacons
> Along the way
> To becoming new.
>
> Anna McKenzie

I think as I write of Beth who at forty is dying a long and tedious death of cancer. Beth has spent a life of drawing short straws for this is her third cancer, and now, unable to wait for her to die, her man has gone off with another woman. Oh, Beth's had her pockets well and truly emptied and she prays, like Anna:

> And we hate you
> As we love you,
> And our anger is as strong
> As our pain,
> Our grief is deep as oceans,
> And our need as great as mountains.
>
> Anna McKenzie

It's difficult to make any sense of Beth's pain, or indeed of

Katie's either. Katie was thirty-five when she died, though she looked a lot older. She was a woman short-changed from birth, poor in all the good things we take for granted. She died a horrid, foetid death and no one came to see her. Day after day she waited, but the visitors never came: not her mother nor her lovers, not even her children. There was only the anxious social worker who wondered if he ought to bring in her kids to say goodbye or if she'd like to write some edifying little message to them before she died. Poor Katie: I doubt if she ever said anything very edifying to anyone. And yet the nurses loved her and when she died they went in droves to her funeral so that she shouldn't go that last sad journey humiliatingly alone.

It's difficult to know what sense to make of the Katies of this world. Certainly she could wrest no meaning or consolation from her drab life and lonely end. From the way she spoke of it, it seems there was little joy even in the begetting of her children, and certainly none in rearing them.

For others it is mercifully different. They live life with a rare passion and even their dying is full of light and laughter. Lizzie was one of those rare people who shone more and more as her life moved towards its close. She'd spent a long tough time in the desert, including finding her husband dead when she came home from work one day. Not given to complaining, she ignored her failing health and faced each new day with a sense of wonder and gratitude that delighted all who met her. She attended our day care unit at the hospice once or twice a week and was always at the centre of a group of laughing patients and nurses. I remember with particular clarity the day she announced she would give a lecture on perfumes: she had been a beauty consultant and was an expert saleswoman. There we sat – other patients, men and women, a couple of nurses, the matron, a visiting clergyman and myself while she instructed us on which perfumes were good for seduction and whether they should be applied to the lobe of the ear or tantalizingly deep in the cleavage!

As so often happens, her radiance sprang from her own rich personality and a deepening faith in God and a week or so before she died the bishop came to confirm her, to ratify what we knew anyway: that she was already anointed and strengthened for her journey. Lizzie was ready to go all right, her roots had been shaken free of the dry earth to which most of us cling with such painful tenacity.

Perhaps that is the essence of this desert experience, the deep gut level understanding that we have here no abiding city, that we are sojourners in a land we did not make. The dying are like refugees, like any homeless people, rootless and insecure, vulnerable and afraid.

Jesus saw this insecurity as a condition for discipleship, for he told a man who wanted to follow him, 'Foxes have holes and the birds of the air have nests, but the Son of Man has nowhere to lay his head.'[1]

What did he mean here, I wonder, for earlier on he invited a prospective disciple to come home with him and see where he lived. Perhaps he was now at a much more dangerous and itinerant stage of his mission, moving quickly along the road and sleeping in a different bed each night lest the Pharisees lay hands on him.

I was reminded starkly of this way of life this summer when I spent some time with a missionary friend from Chile; we had not seen each other for nearly fifteen years and spoke with speed and intensity of times shared and of mutual friends. When I asked her when she had last spoken with Ita Ford and Carla she told me that she'd visited Salvador on impulse in June 1980, just five months before Ita died. It was not an easy visit for she didn't know where they were and travelling around was difficult and dangerous. Eventually she met up with a Latin American sister who offered to drive her to the coast where she found her two friends and they spent an evening together. When I asked about the friendly nun, she said, 'Oh she went off; she never spent the night in the same place: it was too dangerous.'

For sisters Ita Ford and Carla Piette, Maryknoll's 'David and Jonathan' their first months in El Salvador were a profound experience of rootlessness. After many years of working together in Chile they had parted and, each discerning quite separately, had made their decision to come to El Salvador in response to Archbishop Romero's request for foreign priests and religious to help his beleaguered Church.

It was Carla who made her decision first, after visiting the country from her reconnoitre base in Nicaragua. Visiting two Maryknoll Sisters based in Santa Ana, she put her hand deep into El Salvador's wounded side, touching for herself the appalling living conditions of the people, and the violence and terror in the air, with its stories of mutilated bodies, kidnappings and general lawlessness. Listening to the Archbishop's voice as he broadcast his Sunday sermon Carla was impressed by 'his great holiness and love for the truth', and knew she wanted to work in Salvador, whatever the risks. 'I like this place with its spunky people', she wrote, '. . . and now the top is about to blow off – and with reason.' Meanwhile, Ita, still in Chile, was discerning whether she too should answer the call for sisters to go to El Salvador. After a final period of prayer she made her decision and wrote to her mother that she felt 'good with the decision to go'. With characteristic laconic wit she wrote, 'I realize this isn't the greatest news I've ever given you but I think it's a good decision. I'll also be a continent nearer.'

On St Patrick's Day, 17 March 1980, Ita called Nicaragua from Chile to tell Carla and her other friends that she too would be coming to Salvador. Just seven days later Carla left the safety of the newly democratic Nicaragua for what she described as a 'concentrated little bouillon cube of a country', to throw in her lot with the Salvadoran Church and its people. She looked forward in particular to meeting and working with the Archbishop who had become such an inspiration to all Christians caught up in the Latin American struggle and who had spoken so prophetically on their behalf in Belgium as he received the Nobel Prize for Peace:

> I am a shepherd who, with his people, has begun to learn a beautiful and difficult truth: our Christian faith requires that we submerge ourselves in this world . . .
>
> The world that the Church must serve is the world of the poor, and the poor are the ones who decide what it means for the Church to really live in the world . . .
>
> It is the poor who force us to understand what is really taking place . . . the persecution of the Church is a result of defending the poor. The poor are the body of Christ today. Through them he lives on in history . . .

Did Carla know, as the Archbishop clearly knew, that he was at grave personal risk because of his constant and public stand against the government? I don't know. Perhaps the idea of the assassination of an archbishop was too monstrous to entertain, although he himself had spoken publicly about it only three weeks before when he said in an interview with a Mexican newspaper, 'My life has been threatened many times. I have to confess that, as a Christian, I don't believe in death without resurrection. If they kill me I will rise again in the Salvadoran people.'

However much Carla knew that this might happen, the reality, when it came, was catastrophic. Arriving in San Salvador by bus from Nicaragua on the evening of Monday 24 March, the eve of the feast of the Annunciation, Carla drove with her friend the two and a half hour journey to Santa Ana, only to learn that the Archbishop had died while they were on the road, shot at the altar as he said mass in the chapel of the little hospital where he had his room.

The next day the three sisters returned to the capital and Carla wrote to friends at Maryknoll, 'Here I am sitting on the steps of the Cathedral in San Salvador where the body of Archbishop Romero has been brought in silent procession from the Basilica. The sadness that slowly settles over a people at the death of a father, pastor, guide and prophet is the sadness that Salvador is now wrapped in.'

This sadness and fear was to spread like a pall over El Salvador, trapping many of its people in a state akin to shock. This quasi-paralysis was to make life extremely difficult for Ita and Carla as they struggled to integrate themselves in the country and find out where they could best work. In the weeks following the Archbishop's assassination six priests left the country and those who were left behind were overworked and largely silent in the face of the persecution which continued unabated. Ita (who had arrived a week after the Archbishop's death) wrote with Carla: 'the constant violation of human rights by the state and security forces, produces, from our observations, a type of state of shock among the Salvadoran pastoral agents, as well as frustration and impotence caused by the silence of the hierarchical Church.'

The next few weeks were spent in getting to know the country and investigating where best they should work until, towards the end of May, they met with senior members of the archdiocese and it was decided that they should work with the refugees in the area of Chalatenango, in the north of the country. Father Cesar Jerez, the Superior of the Jesuits in Central America, met them at this time and confirmed that their decision was a good one. I love his description of them: 'I admired Carla and Ita's dedication; their simplicity and their commitment, the one rather large like the strong woman in the Gospel, the other fragile, like a reed in the desert.'

In settling on Chalatenango as their base for ministry Ita and Carla were not governed by prudence but by the raw needs of the people. Nor did they go there under any illusions for in one of the towns they visited, twenty-five people had been murdered and the security forces would not allow their bodies to be buried. Carla wrote starkly of the experience: 'So the families of the twenty-five people watched them being eaten by vultures and a typhoid epidemic is in full swing.'

Familiar as I am with the cruelty of a repressive regime and the reality of torture and political killings I find the brutality of life in Salvador difficult to comprehend. For Ita and Carla too, submerged as they were in the people's world, the reality was hard to believe. They clearly received in full, however, the grace to accept their call with open arms and hearts. I am reminded in this context of a remarkable piece of wisdom from Dietrich Bonhoeffer who wrote,

> I believe that God can and will bring good out of evil, even out of the greatest evil. For that purpose he needs men who make the best use of everything. I believe that God will give us all the strength we need to resist in all times of distress. But he never gives it in advance, lest we rely on ourselves and not on him alone.[2]

Ita's deep interior peace in the midst of the storms around her is apparent in these words written on 1 June:

> I don't know if it is in spite of, or because of the horror, terror, evil, confusion, lawlessness, but I do know that it is right to be here, to activate our gifts, to use them in this situation, to believe that we are gifted in and for Salvador now, and that the answers to the questions will come when they are needed. To walk in faith one day at a time with the Salvadorans along a road filled with obstacles, detours and sometimes washouts – this seems to me what it means

> to be for us in El Salvador. It's a privilege to come to a Church of martyrs and people with a strong committed faith.[3]

If I didn't have confidence in the truthfulness of my sources as I transcribe this passage I would be tempted to think it had been written in hindsight by a disciple more intent upon bringing out the meaning of these women's ultimate deaths than upon historical accuracy. It seems too much of a coincidence that Carla was to die within three months when a road was washed away while Ita herself would be murdered on a lonely road deliberately blocked by an obstacle.

It was on the day that this passage was written that my friend Sister Jane Kenrick met up with Ita and Carla in the house of the Cleveland Diocesan Mission to El Salvador, sharing supper and much talk with the two women and their new friend, lay missioner Jean Donovan from Cleveland, Ohio. Listening to Jane's account of her visit brought me one step nearer to understanding how it was for Ita and Carla during those last months for she told me two things in particular: of the incredible loneliness of the deserted road from the airport to Santa Ana, and how Ita had said that maybe that was the last time they would meet because the place they were going to was very dangerous.

And so it was that Ita and Carla began their new ministry as the Emergency Committee for the Vicariate of Chalatenango. Sharing a room in the convent of some other sisters, they spent much of their time on the road, ferrying refugees, food or medical supplies. Chalatenango is a mountainous area with a peasant population of around 200,000 people scattered in small villages over the 2,000 square kilometres. It was also an area in which the peasants' unions had been active and as a result many of the villages had been raided by the security forces who tortured, mutilated and killed many people, particularly the leaders of the Christian communities. By the time Ita and Carla arrived many of the people had fled in terror to the hills or escaped into neighbouring Honduras. It was these refugees from the ravaged villages who had to be fed and comforted and transported to various parish houses and centres where they could be cared for. This is

Carla's description of their work – a far cry from the archetypal image of the life of the nun.

> This may seem strange to you, but as the repression and genocide continue, it becomes harder and harder to do pastoral work. So what do I do? I drive people places – like other sisters who are more and more afraid to stay in the isolated parts of the country areas – I drive Caritas food to refugees of which there are 2,000 families in the department of Chalatenango. I go to meetings where needs are expressed and frustrations aired and in general very little accomplished. I have come to appreciate what Jesus means when he says 'I am the Way'. The way here is daily changing as one tries to respond to this genocidal situation. In one parish where there are no longer any priests or sisters because of the situation, there were forty-two adult catechists – all forty-two have been brutally murdered. No one wants to be a catechist any more since it usually means your life and yet we try to attend to these remote parts of the country . . .

And even after this, Carla was still able to say, 'I believe in the Lord of the Impossible.' But even this rock-like faith didn't protect both Carla and Ita from the loneliness and insecurity of their situation. Their lack of their own home and of friends and colleagues with whom they could share made life very difficult indeed, as we see from this cry from the heart:

> For the last three months we have had no house of which we could say, 'This is our home . . . '. We are pastoral workers used to having people with whom we can visit, meet with etc. Now we have no people – we cannot visit because of the times and the very real fear of placing others in danger because of belonging to the church, which is one of the security forces' biggest enemies. Besides lacking our own home, a stable salary, local church and tangible regional support, and inventing a job daily, neither of us is an emotional or psychological giant in this crazy situation. We realize that a lot of our energies just go into trying to keep walking down this dark road without becoming as dark as the situation.

Foxes have their holes and the birds have their nests, but this David and Jonathan, like their Lord, had nowhere to lay their heads. The road to Jerusalem can be very dark indeed.

As the storm clouds gathered and persecution of the Church increased after Archbishop Romero's death, Ita and Carla became increasingly aware that they too might be killed: 'Carla and I had talked lots of times about the possibility of our dying because of things here, very violent things. We talked about how difficult it would be if we weren't together for the one who was left behind.' More afraid perhaps of this loneliness than of anything else, Ita had asked a friend to pray that if she and Carla were to be killed, that they should die together. It seems a small enough request, in the circumstances, but 'The Lord does whatever he wills', and it seems that it was 'written' that Carla should die first. On Thursday 21 August, 1980, when the two women had been in Salvador for about five months, Carla took a couple of days off to pray and reflect. Before she left, she and Ita prayed together and read a favourite passage from Ezekiel, 'I will take away your hearts of stone and give you hearts of flesh!'[4]

'God has already done that for me,' Carla told Ita and then told her of the time, years before in Chile, when she had prayed for a heart of stone.

'I've come miles since then and you've walked a lot of that road with me,' Carla went on and then, moved by whatever intuition we will never know, she prayed.

'Now you can dismiss your servant in peace, O Lord.'

Ita, it seems, misunderstood her and responded with a quip.

'I'm not sure I get dismissed so easily.' Carla, however, was serious, and responded quietly, 'We'll see!'[5]

Carla spent her two days in San Salvador where she was able to visit Archbishop Romero's grave to pray. She returned home on the Friday evening and spent the following day with a local priest visiting groups of peasants, celebrating the Eucharist and delivering supplies of food and first aid materials.

Ita, meanwhile, went to visit the colonel at the local army base to present him with a list of people who had recently gone missing, so that the authorities might possibly think twice about making them 'disappear' for ever. Perverse as ever, he released a prisoner into her custody, a man who turned out to have betrayed his neighbours to the security forces. The moment the other refugees in the parish centre saw the man they were afraid. Their husbands and sons had been killed the week before and they saw this man as a traitor who would betray their whereabouts to the authorities.

Wearily, Ita and Carla decided they'd better take him home that night and set out in the jeep, with two seminarians to make the half-hour journey to where he lived.

Not knowing the terrain of Chalatenango, it is difficult to visualize what happened during the ensuing fifteen to twenty minutes. This is Ita's description, 'We were just about ten minutes outside of Chalatenango when one of those really freaky, heavy rains began. We had the choice of two roads, one has no rivers along it but had had a lot of landslides (and we thought) the other was the better way to go, the one where you cross the El Chapote River about five times.'

They crossed the river four times but by the time they came to the fifth the water had risen so much Carla knew it was too dangerous to cross. Leaving their passenger to make the final crossing on his own Carla turned the jeep round and headed for home only to find that the place where they had forded the stream just five minutes earlier was now a raging torrent four feet deep. Just what happened next I can't quite work out but the jeep was caught by the water and pulled into the torrent. Frantically, they tried to get out but the jeep turned over on the driver's side, the door closed and the water poured in.

Carla, the clown, the strong woman, managed to shove her friend through the window, but she herself was caught by the black and turbulent water.

> Then would the waters have engulfed us,
> the torrent gone over us.
> Over our head would have swept
> the raging waters.
>
> Psalm 123

Ita, too, carried rapidly down the river, found herself going under and said, 'I'm ready, Lord, receive me!' For three kilometres she struggled in the water until suddenly she found herself clinging to some roots, listening to a voice which told her that she had to get out of the river. Thirty or forty times Ita struggled to haul herself painfully up the high and muddy river bank but eventually she made it, and after blundering about in the dark among the corn stalks she collapsed under a bush.

All night, she lay there, bitten incessantly by the mosquitoes until, around six o'clock in the morning, she heard again the cry of rescuers. This time she found the strength to make her way towards them.

> I got myself up and started making my way down the mountain. When I got to the river bank I started to call and some man came along and I said, 'Did you hear what they were saying? I'm one of those people.' So he crossed the river, took me home to his house and gave me a towel to put around me and we started to walk towards the town.

While Ita was revived and her wounds tended, the search continued for Carla, until around noon they found her, 'Her broken, twisted, naked body had been washed up on a sand bar in the now tame river, fourteen kilometres from where the jeep had foundered the night before.'

So now, Carla was dead. The very situation which Ita had prayed to be spared had happened and she knew she must continue alone. Her one concern, that first day, was Carla's funeral. Refusing offers from the city she insisted that Carla be buried in Chalatenango among the people that she had served and that the readings should be Romans 8: 'Nothing can separate us from the love of God' and the Gospel of John: 'Greater love hath no man than to lay down his life for his friends'.

And so, on 25 August, Carla was buried in her rainbow dress and without her shoes because otherwise she would not have fitted in the five foot eight inch coffin. The church was packed with people come to bid her farewell, and even those refugees on the death lists crept quietly into the chapel to pay their respects. Then, they took her down the long hill to the entrance to the town and to the cemetery. The road was muddy and slippery after the heavy rain and Ita had to hang on to the coffin from behind lest it slide down the hill. She wrote afterwards, 'It occurred to me that this would be the last time I'd ever have to try to hold Carla back.'

Lord of our troubled world:
We pray for all who suffer,
for refugees and orphans,
for families disrupted by war.
We pray for church workers and missionaries,
for all who work with the afflicted.
Help us to work for justice,
without which we have no right to peace.

Note: The Anna McKenzie poem quoted in this chapter is printed in full in the appendix.

6

A Party in Bethany

Over this dead loss to society
You pour your precious ointment.
Sydney Carter

Six days before the Passover, and just under two thousand years before Oscar Romero was shot dead (like Ghandi) during evening prayers, Jesus of Nazareth went to a party. It was a smallish party, as far as we can gather, given by some close friends of his, Lazarus and his two sisters Mary and Martha who lived in Bethany, two miles outside Jerusalem. We know rather more about this family than about Jesus' other friends: perhaps because he saw a lot of them, maybe stayed with them when he was on his way to Jerusalem, when he went up there to preach.

Not long before, Jesus and his friends had been dramatically caught up together because Lazarus had died and, four days later, when he was already in the tomb, Jesus had brought him back to life. How is it, I wonder, that we can read this mind-boggling story without our hair standing on end and our spines chilling? 'You must be joking', we should be saying, 'you're kidding me, making it up.' And yet, there it is baldly written down: 'The dead man came out, his feet and hands bound with bands of stuff and a cloth around his face. Jesus said to them, "Unbind him, let him go free".'[1]

What happened next, I wonder? Did the women faint? Did people prostrate themselves on the floor in adoration? And then what? Did Jesus go away or did he stay with them and debrief them? My guess is he stayed around for a while and maybe they all talked about it together. Or perhaps they were too scared or overawed to mention it and Martha fussed about making Lazarus something to eat or cooking supper for whoever was around.

But what about Mary, the one who'd sat adoringly at Jesus' feet, hanging on his every word while her sister prepared the dinner? Had she become especially close to Jesus, perhaps had time to talk to him alone? And if she did, had he confided in her that he was afraid of what the future would bring? This seems to me important for although we pay lip service to the fact that Jesus was a man like ourselves we never *really* think of him as having to do battle with the darker side of life, with doubt, temptation, exhaustion, irritability and fear. We know, of course, that he was tempted in the desert – but the way these temptations are portrayed in the Gospel makes it hard for us to identify with Jesus. After all, we are not tempted to turn stones into bread but rather to eat too much cake, or to take more than our fair share of whatever cake is on offer, be it land or money or time or sexual gratification. Perhaps it would be easier for us to love ourselves and our brothers if we thought that Jesus sometimes wanted to stay in bed rather than go out to preach the gospel or that he had nearly had an affair with Mary Magdalen. Leaving the issue of these carnal temptations on one side, I cannot believe that Jesus did not suffer from weariness and mood swings or the occasional free floating anxiety (what Holly Golightly – Truman Capote's heroine in *Breakfast at Tiffanys* – so vividly describes as the 'mean reds!'). So, I hereby offer my hypothesis that Jesus of Nazareth, Emmanuel, God with us, having humbled himself to share in our humanity, was not immune to the 'mean reds' and that Mary of Bethany was one of his friends in whom he confided.

All of which leads us back to the dinner party which Martha and Mary and Lazarus held for Jesus, perhaps to celebrate Lazarus' recovery. (Why, oh why, I say to myself, does the Lazarus story not figure in the Synoptic Gospels? Didn't they know about it? Or did John make it up? When I ask questions like that I'm told not to be a fundamentalist and I protest in fury that I'm not. But it does seem to be a very remarkable story for John to have made up just to prove a theological point that Jesus had conquered death. Enough. If you want to look into that, go and find yourself a Scripture scholar because I certainly don't pretend to be one.)

John tells us quite clearly that the raising of Lazarus was the last straw for the Pharisees and that when they heard about it they said, 'Enough is enough! Here is this man working all these signs, and what action are we taking? If we let him go on in this way everybody will believe in him and the Romans will come and destroy the Holy Place and our nation.' It was then that Caiaphas, the high priest of the year, suggested that Jesus should be killed, because it was better for one man to die than for the people to be scattered. So, John tells us, 'From that day they were determined to kill him. So Jesus no longer went about openly among the Jews, but left the district for a town called Ephraim, in the country bordering on the desert, and stayed there with his disciples.'[2]

It seems, then, that Jesus came out of hiding to visit his friends and that to do so was risky. He knew, too, that his time was approaching, and he must surely have been deeply afraid. When I think of Jesus at this party I think of all the people who have to conceal how they feel at public events because it would not be polite or politic to let their hair down. There are the people with AIDS, struggling to hold down a job without letting on that they are ill because they would probably get the sack. How hard that is: and, in a very real sense, we heap this weight upon them because if it was socially acceptable to be dying of AIDS people would not go in fear of being found out. And then there are the gay people who grieve in secret for the death of a lover because it is not socially acceptable in 'polite society' to be in love with someone of the same sex. How hard we make it for those who do not conform to what we, the straight, the righteous, the religious see as OK. It is all right to be a thirty-year-old man dying of lung cancer because you've been wounded or stupid enough to smoke forty cigarettes a day for the past ten years, but it's very definitely not all right to be a thirty-year-old man dying with AIDS because you're gay, wounded or stupid enough to be an intravenous drug abuser and happen to be addicted to heroin rather than nicotine.

Jesus knew he was going to die and yet he smiled and joined in the conversation because that's what polite people do. But Mary knew something that the others didn't know or wouldn't face and she did the only thing she could think of which was to make a massive public declaration of love by pouring a box of expensive embalming ointment over his feet and wiping it off with her hair. I love to imagine the scene, the commotion it must have caused and the pungent smell of the aromatic oils as it spread through the house.

And why did she do it? The commentaries talk about her doing it for Jesus' burial, but I can't say that makes a lot of sense to me. I think Mary wanted to say 'I love you'. I care that you're lonely and afraid. I wish I could stop it happening but I know it's got to be. So here is a SIGN, a sign that I know how you feel, that you are precious to me. My wasting this stuff on you is the only way I know how to make up to you for what you're going through now.

The Bethany story is especially important to many of us who work in the hospice movement for we too pour the precious ointment of our time, our skill and our love over those who are dying and who, therefore, in human terms are of no further economic worth. Let me quote again Sydney Carter's poem which sums up for me the work we do:

> No revolution will come in time
> to alter this man's life
> except the one surprise
> of being loved.
> He has no interest in Civil Rights,
> Neo marxism
> psychiatry
> or any kind of sex.
> He has only twelve more hours to live
> so never mind about
> a cure for smoking, cancer, leprosy,
> or osteo arthritis.
> Over this dead loss to society
> you pour your precious ointment,
> call the bluff
> and laugh at the
> fat and clock faced gravity
> of our economy.
> You wash the feet that
> will not walk tomorrow.
> Come levity of love,
> Show him, show me

in this last step of time
Eternity, leaping and capering.

The more I think about this poem and the more I look at the style of loving that the hospice movement has set, the more convinced I become that it has something to say far beyond the field of the care of the dying. I have written before that the hospice movement stands in a prophetic relationship to mainstream medicine but I am coming to the belief that this movement (and others like it) have a message for the world at large. Let me explain.

The hospice movement (and I would gather in here movements like L'Arche and others which open their homes and their hearts to the poor and the dispossessed) has rediscovered a way or a style of loving which is very close to what Jesus taught. What I mean by this is that there is a certain profligacy of caring that goes beyond the demands of justice and enters the realm of loving. It is not that clients necessarily cross the boundaries that should contain them and enter the space reserved for family but that the clients are treated as if they were family.

Let me illustrate this with the story of David and Mary who entered my life together one Boxing Day morning, (for my American friends, Boxing Day is the day after Christmas Day). I was on duty at the hospice and doing a rather lick and a promise kind of ward round because both the patients and I were suffering the after-effects of a rather over-indulgent Christmas Day when the telephone rang. Perhaps I should explain that we are not an emergency service and we try not to take admissions at the weekends so that the staff can have a bit of a breather, so our defensives were gently raised at the thought of a new patient. The nurse who'd taken the call beckoned to me, however, and with her hand over the receiver said, 'I think you'd better handle this one.' When I picked up the 'phone I saw what she meant for I found myself tuned in to a very angry, very desperate lady who said that her twenty-year-old son, who was dying of a brain tumour, was screaming with pain and could we help.

Now this kind of 'phone call has to be handled with great discretion because such patients are already under the care of their own physicians and to rush immediately to their aid would tread on all sorts of toes and cause chaos in a system which, by and large, works quite well. But this case seemed different: it was a particularly dead time of the year, the patient was very young and his mother was patently at the end of her rope. After listening to her at some length, I rang the boy's doctor and very diffidently offered our services.

From the alacrity with which he accepted my offer I should have known that this was going to be a tricky one but as I had said, it was the season of goodwill and I was off guard. Having blackmailed a reluctant ambulance service (they were on strike for all except emergencies) to set out at once on a three-hour drive across the moors, I went off to salvage what I could of the holiday.

Six hours later Mary and her boy were installed and the patient oxes and asses had moved up to accommodate them (we don't normally admit patients' relatives but there seemed no way we could detach this woman from her son and, anyway, she had no money and was in no state to drive home). Little by little, as I listened to her story, I began to understand why she was so desperate. David, it seemed, had been ill for two years. At first the doctors pooh-poohed his symptoms, attributing them to malingering or anxiety about forthcoming exams. Eventually, however, a brain tumour was diagnosed and despite surgery and radiotherapy the tumour had returned and was taking over David's brain like a pillaging army. It was only when we came to know Mary well over the coming weeks that we were able to understand the magnitude of the tragedy for here was a particularly gifted young man, a musician and a composer and, much more important, he was very, very nice.

By the time we met him, David's tumour had spread to both sides of his brain producing a rare and dramatic disability: short-term memory loss. This meant that in the space of a few minutes, he completely forgot what had been said to him. We see a lot of patients with brain tumours in the course of our work at the hospice and many of them have quite severe mental impairment but mercifully, this is often more distressing for the relatives than for the patients themselves. For David, however, things were different, for it made it quite impossible to give him any kind of lasting comfort, to help him to achieve a state of peace of mind. Looking Mary straight in the eye, he would ask, 'Am I going to die?' Holding his hand, she would answer, 'Yes darling, I'm afraid you are.' Apparently digesting this information for a few moments he would ask 'When?' and she would reply, 'Darling, we're not sure – maybe quite soon.' We could see this terrible information sinking in, and then running out as if out of a colander, for after a minute or so elapsed he would enquire again: 'Am I going to die?'

It does not require a very active imagination to see what this kind of experience would do to a mother. I think this Mary's heart had a lot more than seven sword thrusts and it was some kind of miracle that she held together as well as she did.

For the next six weeks they lived with us, as near a part of our family as any patient can be. Mary shared David's room and rarely left him. We discovered she was a painter and encouraged her to set up her easel so while David slept or listened to his music she painted furiously, lovely green pictures full of bright grass and leaves with splodges of pink or purple flowers.

After about five days had elapsed and we thought they were well settled, Mary announced suddenly that she was taking David home. Wondering what had gone wrong, we enquired gently as to why she felt she must go and discovered that David was missing his dog and she felt she should take him home so they could be together. Laughing, we said, 'If that's all that's worrying you, go and get him. We'd love to have a dog around.' Mary looked at us disbelievingly but eventually went off and in the evening returned with the most enormous red setter I have ever seen! David was overjoyed, and after that there was no more talk of going home and we became used to the sight of David lying asleep in one bed and Robin lying, one ear cocked, on guard, on the other! I remember with much laughter the day when I popped in to see David and found that Mary had gone out to lunch. As I approached my patient's bed, I heard a low growl from the other bed and decided that I would defer my visit to a time when Mary was on duty rather than Robin!

I tell this story partly because it's a lovely story anyway, but also to illustrate the way in which the dying can be cared for if we choose to make the resources available to them.

David would have received good medical and loving nursing care in his local hospital: of that I have no doubt. But, because we have the resources, and because we have forgotten a little how 'proper' doctors and nurses behave we were able to offer a quite different kind of welcome to David and his mother. We were able to go that extra mile to give to Mary what we would want for ourselves: 'Judge not, and you will not be judged; condemn not, and you will not be condemned; forgive, and you will be forgiven; give and it will be given to you; good measure, pressed down, shaken together, running over will be put into your lap. For the measure you give will be the measure you get back.'[3]

Jesus said quite clearly that he did not come to destroy the law, but to build upon it. He came to show, by his teaching and by example, that there is a better way to love: a scandalous way in which the lonely are scooped up and cherished, sinners are forgiven and the poor have their baskets filled to overflowing. There is a wideness in the mercy and a lavishness in the loving of God that we are challenged to emulate.

And of course, people do emulate it, many many people in all sorts of areas of caring. You meet it in organizations for the mentally handicapped, for the homeless, for the elderly and for patients with Altzheimers and those with AIDS. But this kind of caring is not yet the norm, perhaps because it is a very costly kind of loving.

Lord of the Universe, Master of All,
look in love upon your people.
Pour the healing oil of your compassion
on a world that is wounded and dying.
Send us out in search of the lost,
to comfort the afflicted,
to bind up the broken,
and to free those trapped
under the rubble of their fallen dreams.

7

Last Suppers

Somewhere someone is travelling
furiously towards you,
At incredible speed, travelling day
and night,
Through blizzards and desert heat,
across torrents, through narrow passes.
But will he know where to find you,
Recognize you when he sees you,
Give you the thing he has for you?

John Ashberry *At North Farm*

On 1 December 1980, the night before she died, Ita Ford attended a farewell dinner. She was in good heart, for she was among friends and the dark cloud that had settled over her after Carla's death had begun to lift. The occasion was the last day of the Maryknoll Sisters' annual Regional Assembly and it was held in a retreat house in Managua in Nicaragua. There were twenty-two Maryknoll sisters from Central America: from Panama, Nicaragua, and El Salvador, and two guests from war-torn Guatemala.

Forgive me if I digress for a moment and tell you about the Maryknoll Sisters for they are a unique group of women who have a very special place in my heart. As a congregation, they were started in 1911 by a woman called Mary Rogers to work alongside the Maryknoll Fathers, a group of American priests formed to serve in the Foreign Missions. Their mother house in Ossining, New York, high above the Hudson River, is an amazing place where I have stayed on a number of occasions. It's only there that you get a real feel for the breadth of work that these women do, for they serve not only in Latin and Central America, but also in Africa and the East, India, China, Korea and Japan.

My clearest memory of 'the Knoll' as it is affectionately known is the dining room, an enormous cafeteria where over fifty women sit around quietly talking at small tables, dressed in anything from Bermuda shorts to the full religious habit. There is a matter of factness about their demeanour which deceives the untutored onlooker for they look like any group of women, nurses, schoolteachers or whatever. But if you sit around for a while you'll find yourself being introduced to people, 'this is Peg; she got back from Chile yesterday', or 'this is Mary, she's just home from Korea'. And you find that these very ordinary looking women spent yesterday on the plane and the day before in some wooden shack working alongside refugees or mothers whose babies are dying of malnutrition. Sometimes it's the other way round and you suddenly miss a familiar face and someone says, 'Oh – you mean Bernie – she left this morning at six.' And you discover that Bernie's gone back to Central America or wherever her mission is and she won't be back for a couple of years unless her mother dies, or she gets very ill or something unexpected happens.

So the meeting in Nicaragua was special, a reunion of old friends, of sisters in the spirit who knew very well they might not see each other again. At the close of the meeting they prayed and Ita read a passage from one of Archbishop Romero's homilies: 'Christ invites us not to fear persecution because, believe me brothers and sisters, one who is committed to the poor must risk the same fate as the poor. And in El Salvador we know what the fate of the poor signifies: to disappear, to be tortured, to be captive and to be found dead.'[1]

When I wrote earlier about the 'space' between the Kairos moment of option for a dangerous mission and death I likened it to a desert, bleak and inhospitable but with oases of good talk and laughter. This party, like Jesus' last supper, was such an oasis. Ita, having talked in depth about her grief at Carla's death and having been able to share it with friends who had known Carla well, was able to join in with a verve which she had found impossible earlier in the week. She surprised everyone by volunteering to be in one of the skits and later jumped up to teach the 'barnyard shuffle' as the group sang 'Old MacDonald had a farm' and Maura Clarke, the gentle, rather timid sister who had only lately found the courage to replace Carla in Chalatenango, joined in the merriment by dancing the Irish jig.

Meanwhile, Jean Donovan, lay missioner from Cleveland who was to die with Ita and Maura the following day, was also at a party, with Robert White, the US ambassador to Salvador, and his wife Mary Anne. This, too, was a merry party, and Jean was clearly enjoying herself, declaring, 'this is terrific, I haven't had a glass of scotch in a long time.'[2]

How important it is that we remember that Ita Ford danced the barnyard shuffle and that Jean Donovan drank a glass of scotch the night before they died because it helps us to earth the 'Last Supper' in our own time and place. Jesus of Nazareth held a party the night before he died and like Ita's and Jean's his laughter must have rung out under the stars.

There was serious conversation, too, for all of them, for they knew full well the risks they were running. Jesus had spoken about it many times: 'Now we are going up to Jerusalem, and the Son of Man is about to be handed over to the chief priests and scribes. They will condemn him to death and will hand him over to the pagans to be mocked and scourged and crucified . . . '[3]

Ita, too, knew that her life was in terrible danger. At the meeting, she explained that, because of the stand that the archdiocese had taken against injustice, the Church 'is encountering a notable increase in hostility and incidents that indicate a fore-meditated persecution. From January through October 1980 there have been twenty-eight assassinations of Church personnel, three woundings, twenty-one arrests, four profanations of the Eucharist, forty-one machine gunnings of Church buildings, fourteen bombings, and thirty-three search and seizures of Church properties.'[4]

It is difficult for us who see violence only on our television screens to understand how it was for this fragile reed of a woman, so recently bereaved of her closest friend, to contemplate returning to such a situation. That she found it increasingly difficult to continue is apparent from the account of her conversations with Maryknoll psychiatrist Sister Maria Rieckelman who had come down from the United States to attend the Regional Assembly. At the Thanksgiving dinner on 26 November she was withdrawn and distracted, unable to enter into the festivities and she told Maria, 'I really don't feel very thankful.' She talked to Maria of Carla's death and the situation in El Salvador and how hard it was to be constantly among people who were burying their dead or looking for missing family members. She spoke of going to an open grave with a mother to look for her son and said, 'I could not do that again.'

Jean, too, the pragmatic flippant Jeanie, knew that her life was in danger and she had suffered deeply during September when she was home on leave and had the time and space to reflect.

> Death was not so much of a fear as was torture. That was one terror for her. One of the last things she said was, 'I just hope I'm not found on a ditch bank with all the markings of torture.' She didn't know when it was going to happen, she just knew. We all did. We all knew. Because Jeanie wouldn't run from a situation – she wouldn't leave people who needed her because it was dangerous. She was a person who walked out on a limb. To stay there was to die.[5]

During her stay in Maryknoll Jean fought with her terror and eventually arrived at a deep peace, such that she was able to write to a friend just two weeks before she died: 'Several times I have decided to leave El Salvador. I almost could except for the children, the poor, bruised victims of this insanity. Who would care for them? Whose heart could be so staunch as to favour the reasonable thing in a sea of their tears and loneliness? Not mine, dear friend, not mine.'[6]

These last suppers are important not just because they reassure us, unnervingly, of the humanity of those who died but because they were occasions on which important things were said. Revellers facing death may laugh and dance but they also have a deep need to communicate what is important to them, what is deep in their hearts. Ita expressed such feelings in a letter to her niece Jennifer on her sixteenth birthday: 'What I want to say, some of it isn't too jolly birthday talk, but it's real. Yesterday I stood looking down at a sixteen-year-old who'd been killed a few hours earlier. I know a lot of kids even younger who are dead. This is a terrible time in El Salvador for youth. A lot of idealism and commitment are getting snuffed out here and now.

'The reason why so many people are being killed is quite complicated, yet there are some clear, simple strands. One is that many people have found a meaning to live, to sacrifice, to struggle and even to die and whether their life spans sixteen years, sixty or ninety, for them their life has had a purpose. In many ways they are fortunate people.

'Brooklyn is not passing through the drama of El Salvador, but some things hold true wherever one is, and at whatever age. What I am saying is that I hope you can come to find that which gives life a deep meaning for you, something that energizes you, enthuses you, enables you to keep moving ahead.

'I can't tell you what it might be. That's for you to find, to choose, to love. I can just encourage you to start looking, and support you in the search' (letter to Jennifer, 16 August 1980).

This letter was Ita's birthday present to Jennifer: in lieu of records, books or perhaps a new dress. In some ways, this letter is less moving than some of the much headier, heavier things Ita wrote to her friends, but in other ways it is more important. It's important because of its simplicity and universality: the application of truths learned on the battlefield to a comfortable sixteen-year-old living in times of peace.

A year or so ago, when I was preparing a lecture on Coping with Spiritual Needs of the Dying, I asked a Jesuit friend how he understood the term 'Spiritual Needs'. He thought for a long while and then gave me his list, prominent among which was the need for a *meaning in life*. People find this vital, intangible entity in many ways: in the love of and for their children, in the service of others or in creating something original or beautiful. But always, nearly always, a meaning in life is caught up in love of another.

It is hardly surprising then, that Jesus' most urgent message, on the night before he died was this:

> My little children,
> I shall not be with you much longer . . .
> I give you a new commandment:

love one another;
just as I have loved you,
you must also love one another.
By this love you have for one another,
everyone will know that you are my disciples.[7]

I find it really quite bizarre, sometimes, when I think how far the Christian Church has strayed away from this fundamental message of the gospel. Jesus did not say that his followers would be known by their purity, by their ascetic behaviour, by their piety or by their distinctive dress but by the love they have for one another.

He even did a role-play (to be strictly accurate, a modelling!) of how they should behave: he poured water into a bowl and, tying a towel around his waist, he went round and washed his disciples' feet. What was he saying, with this dramatic symbolism, almost as flamboyant as Mary of Bethany with the ointment, at the previous week's party? We know quite well what he was saying but, somehow, we forget. He was showing us that loving is inseparable from service and that we must not stand on our dignity but must humble ourselves and do menial, earthy, bodily tasks for our brothers. To put it bluntly, he was saying we must feed the hungry and clothe the naked – and not only that: we must clear the drunkard's throat of vomit and turn him on his side so that he does not choke and we must clear up the foul excreta of those whose bodies are so ravaged by disease that they cannot care for themselves. By *this* shall people know we are his disciples, not by veils or dog collars, cathedrals or statues to the virgin.

The curious thing is that although we all know this, although we've learned it at our mother the Church's knee, we and she somehow forget and have to re-learn it. We have to re-learn it, not so much in theory but in our own situation. It's not that we are all called to go off and be killed in Salvador or to work with refugees in Cambodia but that we are all, all called to find out who are the poor, the hungry and the lonely in our own patch and somehow become involved in washing their feet.

One of the fascinating spin-offs from the hospice movement is the way in which an increasing number of ordinary people are being drawn into caring for the dying on a voluntary basis. In the hospice where I work we have the usual core of paid professional staff: nurses, doctors, social workers, administrators, secretaries and the like. These paid workers form about one quarter of those who work at the hospice – the rest, around two hundred men, women and children, are volunteers, by which I mean they work without pay. Hospice volunteers come in all shapes and sizes, from the school children who come in one afternoon a week to serve the teas, to the consultant physician who has worked one weekend a month for the past eight years. There is Sister Josephine, the Benedictine nun who serves on reception two days a week and works in the kitchen on Saturdays when it's hard to get helpers; and there's Jill, a young widow who is always there manning the 'phone at Christmas and on public holidays when there's just no one else around. There are the gardeners, the handymen, the drivers, and the shop people: all working quietly away in the background so that things run smoothly for the rest of us. Another very interesting group are those who actually pay to come to evening classes so that they may give up their free time to work for nothing: those who are learning to be bereavement counsellors. Last night I lectured to twenty women, who had come to the hospice after a day's work to learn how they might accompany the bereaved, voluntarily entering into their darkness to share the pain of their loss.

I could go on forever: about the ladies who sort the donated clothes that we sell in our shop, and the men and women who go round the pubs collecting money, or stand patiently on street corners rattling tins on a Saturday afternoon. Sometimes all this seems a small miracle when one thinks of how most of us like to spend our free time. And yet they, like us who are paid to care, find that, paradoxically, in giving they receive far more than they'd ever dreamt. It's not just the gratitude of the patients and their families, or even the sense of a job well done. It is, I believe, the joy in service freely given, a joy that one only discovers by doing it. This is what Ita Ford was trying to tell her niece Jennifer when she wrote: 'Hope you can come to find that which gives life a deep meaning for you, something that energizes you, enthuses you, enables you to keep moving ahead. I can't tell you what it might be. That's for you to find, to choose, to love.'

Lord Jesus Christ,
Son of the Living God,
Comforter of widows,
Washer of feet,
show us how to care for each other.
Teach us to love as you did:
Unconditionally, unilaterally,
without fear or favour,
pride, or prejudice.
Give us open hearts
and wise minds
and hands that are worthy
to serve in your name.

8

Dark Night

No worst, there is none. Pitched past pitch of grief,
More pangs will, schooled at fore pangs, wilder wring.
Comforter, where, where is your comforting?
Gerard Manley Hopkins

When the Passover supper was over, and all the psalms had been sung, instead of going home to bed, Jesus and his friends left for the Mount of Olives. When they came to a small estate called Gethsemane, they stopped and Jesus, telling the other disciples to wait for him while he prayed, went on a bit further with his closest friends, Peter, James and John. Then, we are told, 'a sudden fear came over him'[1] and he became very distressed.

What happened next? Did he shake, or cry out? Did he weep, as he fought with the tension welling up within him? 'My soul is sorrowful to the point of death', he said, and telling them to stay where they were and keep awake he moved away from them a little and threw himself on the ground to pray.

This terrible night of fear is one of the most precious accounts we have of Jesus for it reveals him to us in all his humanity. We do well to reflect a moment upon this sorrow 'to the point of death' for fear and grief of this magnitude are part of the human condition and are hard to bear. If dwelling upon the passion of Jesus has any purpose at all it must only be that we enter briefly into the anguish of our world and emerge changed, with a greater understanding and a greater depth of compassion for those who suffer.

Jesus was afraid, as men and women facing death are always afraid. He was afraid of pain, afraid of breaking down under torture, afraid of the process of dying and afraid of the unknown, of that dark place which we must all face one day.

> O dark, dark, dark. They all go into the dark,
> The vacant interstellar spaces, the vacant into the vacant,
> The captains, merchant bankers, eminent men of many letters,
> Distinguished civil servants, chairmen of many committees,
> Industrial lords and petty contractors all go into the dark.
>
> T. S. Eliot 'East Coker', *Four Quartets*

Eliot knew all about fear. He understood the terror of the void: the terror of people like Andy who, dying of leukaemia at seventeen, saw death not as a meeting with Jesus nor as a gentle dreamless sleep but as entering some terrifying intergalactic space. He knew too that fear is a chameleon, that it both swirls about like mist, and lurks in the shadows ready to pounce.

> . . . now a new terror has soiled us, which none can avert, none can avoid, flowing under our feet and over the sky;
> Under doors and down chimneys, flowing in at the ear and the mouth and the eye.
> God is leaving us, God is leaving us, more pang more pain than birth or death.
> Sweet and cloying through the dark air
> Falls the stifling scent of despair;
> The forms take shape in the dark air:
> Puss-purr of leopard, footfall of padding bear,
> Palm-pat of nodding ape, square hyaena waiting
> For laughter, laughter, laughter. The Lords of Hell are here.
> They curl around you, lie at your feet, swing and wing through the dark air.
>
> T. S. Eliot *Murder in the Cathedral*

Good Friday people are no strangers to fear. They learn to live with it, to thumb their noses at it and also to confront it face to face in those dark hours of the night when they are alone. For some, perhaps, as for Jesus, there is a particular time when they face it head on, do battle and then, having come to some kind of truce, are able to move on with renewed strength and inner calm.

Hopkins, who writes so vividly of his own dark hours, speaks of

> . . . That night, that year
> Of now done darkness I wretch lay wrestling with (my
> God!) my God.
>
> Gerard Manley Hopkins *Carrion Comfort*

For Hopkins, as for Jesus, the dark night was a night of combat, a struggle with terror, with his inner demons and, in some mysterious way, with God. Perhaps the real meaning of fear is that it is the context, the battleground in which an individual makes their most important gesture, their fiat, their abandonment to God. Jesus, we are told, prayed that the cup should pass from him, that he should not have to drain to the dregs the bitterness of the days and hours to come. Oh, how important this prayer of his, for in making it he sealed his bond with us, gave us permission to barter with God, to say, 'Please, not me, not me. Don't let me die. Please take away this pain. Restore my child to health. Save my lover. Don't let them torture me. Don't let him rape me. Anything, anything, but don't let THAT happen.'

People don't talk much about their dark nights. Such struggles are deeply intimate affairs, both holy and shameful at the same time, involving as they do a certain nakedness, tears, capitulation and ecstasy.

When we look at Jesus' agony at the garden, particularly when it is 'touched up' by pious artists, presented as a deeply moving, meaningful experience, we find it difficult to identify with what is going on. Dark nights, however, are part of being human and take many forms. They may be short and appallingly painful, like some terrible knife wound or amputation, or long and drawn out, with a weariness and desolation that defies description. And, of course, they are not necessarily one-off events, but may recur again and again in different guises over a lifetime. Perhaps for some the letting go into God is accomplished with one stroke of the sword, for others, the ropes must be sawn at with a rusty bread knife until the last thread finally snaps.

Carla Piette's dark night (or one of them, at least) began in Chile, in 1976 shortly after I was released from prison and expelled. Ita's family had come to visit her and perhaps this awakened within Carla a deep longing to see her own family again. 'Family' for Carla was her mother, her sister Betty and brother-in-law Jack, for her father had died suddenly when Carla was six. Just what impact James Piette's untimely death had upon his wife and little daughter we can only speculate but we are told that Carla's childhood was lonely and she never really understood why her mother was so distant. Perhaps Carla, who always saw herself as the clown, was unconsciously concealing her sad heart under a grease-paint smile.

Childhood grief, however, has a way of erupting quite unexpectedly in middle life and Carla's caught her quite unawares.

> She was on a bus one afternoon, returning from the city to La Bandera (the shanty town where she lived and worked), thinking a thousand thoughts, when all of a sudden she was overcome by an understanding of what her mother must have suffered with the birth of a daughter late in life and the death of her husband a few years later. She broke into sobs as if she were alone with no end to her tears. Weeping uncontrollably, she stumbled from the bus and hurried through the dusty streets, unashamed and finally free of the anguish over the distance between herself and her mother.[2]

Shaken by this experience, Carla decided to go home and spend some time with her mother, so taking some overdue leave, she returned unannounced to the USA thinking that she would give her mother a surprise. Alas for Carla, she was too late. Her mother's mind had gone and not only was she unable to recognize her daughter but she had nightmares when Carla slept in the house.

Almost overwhelmed by a grief such as she had never known, Carla went away for a month to consider her future. As it happened, I was in the United States lecturing during that summer of 1976 and tried hard to persuade Carla to break her retreat to come and see me. Wisely, she refused, but sent me a wonderful cryptic note which said something like, 'It's a great thing to be on a journey into the unknown, particularly when you trust the cabbie.'

Just what happened between Carla and God during this retreat, we will probably never know, save that she was able to write that amazing fiat, to abandon herself into God's hands.

> Abandonment is not just a hanging loose.
> It is a letting go.
> It is a severing of the strings by which one
> manipulates,
> controls
> administrates
> the forces in one's life.
> Abandonment is receiving all things the way one receives
> a gift
> with opened hands,
> and opened heart.
> Abandonment to God
> is the climactic point in any man's life.
>
> Anon. in Edward Farrell's
> *Disciples and Other Strangers*

By September of 1976 Carla was back in Chile, but still fragile from the upheavals in her mind and heart. That she was painfully conscious of her vulnerability is shown in this letter to a friend: 'In the end I had to say no to Venezuela because I am too weak, needy and, I guess you'd say, problematic. Home was very hard. I returned a little less than a basket case and have been recovering slowly, learning once again what it means to be poor and dependent.'[3]

I am reminded here of a phrase from the *Preface of Martyrs*, 'You choose the weak and make them strong', for this fragile 'basket case' of a woman who felt too weak to go to a new mission in Venezuela, was, a couple of years later, to opt for the most dangerous mission available, El Salvador, and be likened by the Jesuit provincial to the strong woman of the Bible.

For Carla, her Gethsemane tears were to be shed mainly in the privacy of a Jesuit retreat house, but Ita's was a much more public affair.

It wasn't until over two weeks after Carla's death that Ita finally broke down. It happened at the American Embassy when she went to leave Carla's death certificate. What cruel demons possessed the official there that day I do not know, but she pointed out that 'not only was Carla's name misspelled but that the judge's certification of death was inadequate because it did not mention in what volume and upon what page her death was noted.' Then, as if that were not hard enough, the woman commented, 'Who could ever prove that she is dead?'

'I offered to sign another statement that I personally saw her buried,' Ita wrote to her mother, 'but they said I would have to return to Chalatenango to get official papers with all the seals.'

Ita spent the next few weeks with the Assumption Sisters in San Salvador, trying to make some kind of sense of her grief. Her grieving was particularly lonely because most of the people who knew her and Carla were far away. She wrote:

> It's one of those mysteries to be asked to mourn alone when everyone else with whom Carla shared her life is in Chile, New York, even Bangladesh. What hit me was that there is no one in this country who knows Carla for longer than four months. Already she is a little bit larger than life, a heroine, an 'angel of charity', and I guess it's useless for me to protest that my beat-up old friend is an example of God's strength being manifest in our weakness, His goodness and love through our vessels of clay.[4]

Vessels of clay: we are only earthen vessels, fragile containers of this precious spirit. Ita loved this image and I remember so well the day when, seated on my bedroom floor with her and Carla, I looked into the light of the candle and listened to her read the potter's story from Jeremiah 18.

And now, during these painful months of grieving, the Potter was reworking Ita on his wheel.

At the beginning of October, after spending a couple of weeks in Guatemala in retreat and then with an old friend, Ita returned to Chalatenango, to be exposed once again to the life of terror and daily killings.

> Often, during their trips to campo (country) towns they would come upon bloated bodies on the side of the road. 'The way innocent people, families, children are cut up with machetes and blessed temples of the Lord thrown and

left for the buzzards to feed on seems unbelievable, but it happens every day,' Maura wrote.

On 2 November, the Feast of All Souls, Jean Donovan and two other missionaries went to Chalatenango to visit Ita and take flowers to Carla's grave. That same day Ita was to have an experience of death which hit her especially hard and, some of her friends believe, gave her some terrible premonition of the death she herself was to die. A woman came to the house in deep distress and begged Ita to accompany her to see if a body recently buried was that of her missing son.

Ita and Jean set off with the woman in the jeep to find the farmer who had buried the two teenagers. He was very reluctant to open the grave as his action in burying the bodies had itself been a breach of the law, but, unable to ignore the mother's distress, he agreed. Gently he dug down into the newly turned earth until he came to a white cloth with which he had covered the boy's face. He lifted it off, and the woman, looking down on to the face of her son, thanked him quietly and said, 'Now I know where my son lies. I know he is with God now. I just want him to rest here.'

Whether it was the pain of the situation, a reactivation of her grief over Carla's death, or a premonition about the way she herself was to die, Ita became very upset by the incident. Jean took her home and tried to comfort her, but she remained uncharacteristically distressed for the rest of that day. It was just one month to the day before she herself was killed, and it was a few days after that Madelaine and Terry, two friends who joined Ita and Jean later that day, were to stand, in their turn, looking down into that same dry earth as the dirt was scraped away to reveal the bodies of their friends, Jean Donovan and Ita Ford, Maura Clarke and Dorothy Kazel, who in following Christ, had suffered the same fate as the poor.

Lord of Creation,
moulder of our fragile clay,
Shape us in your image.
Spin us round, if you must
until we're dizzy;
Hollow us out, if you must,

until we're empty
of all that is false and useless.
Fill us daily with living water
that we may carry your life
to a world dying of thirst.

9

Arrest

I tell you most solemnly,
when you were young
you put on your own belt
and walked where you liked;
but when you grow old
you will stretch out your hands
and somebody else will put a belt around you
and take you where you would rather not go.
John 21:18

Arrest, like birth or death, is a watershed time. As Solzhenitsyn puts it, it is an instantaneous, shattering thrust, expulsion, somersault from one state into another. One minute you are a free agent, at liberty to go where you will, to eat, to sleep, to pee when it suits you and the next, you are powerless, an object, a thing to be numbered, photographed, catalogued, and stored away. No wonder we say of prisoners: 'he was put away', or 'detained at her Majesty's pleasure'. Luckily, our present Majesty takes less pleasure in putting people away than certain of her forefathers, but we do it just the same, using her name to make it sound better.

Every now and then, however, we get pulled up short because someone kills themselves in detention. Yesterday it was a boy of fifteen, awaiting sentence for stealing a handbag, who hanged himself in an adult gaol. Why? Why? No doubt he did it when the balance of his mind was disturbed. But do we ask ourselves *why* the balance of his mind was upset? Should we not perhaps have *expected* the delicate clockwork of an adolescent's mind to be deranged by locking him up alone in a prison cell? The authorities were sorry. The lady magistrate was close to tears. She hadn't wanted to lock him up but the law demanded it. Of course he should have gone to an adolescent unit, but you see there were no vacancies. No room at the inn – so a baby is born in a stable. No room in the children's gaol – so a child is locked away in an adult's prison, and becomes so frightened, so confused that he takes his own life. The parents were devastated. The social workers were furious. The prison governor said it should never have happened. But a child lies dead – because he stole a handbag, and because no one sat down and thought what arrest and imprisonment might do to such a troubled youngster.

In Bangkok, the same day, two teenagers are arrested for smuggling drugs. They are distraught. They deny any knowledge of how the drugs got into their luggage but the authorities don't believe them. The seventeen-year-old is sent to an adolescent unit but the eighteen-year-old stays in an adult prison awaiting trial: and if she is found guilty, the sentence is death.

I would not care to be in that girl's shoes, catapulted as she has been from what, no doubt, seemed a merry adventure into a world of terrifying seriousness. Nor yet would I wish to be her captors, struggling unsuccessfully to hold back a tide of lethal drugs sweeping across their country, leaving devastation and death in its wake. What should they do? Where *should* they detain those stupid girls? *How* should they punish them? Probably they haven't the time or energy to think about preventing their suicide other than taking away their belts and shoe-laces like any sensible gaoler.

How, I wonder, was arrest for Jesus? At least he was adult, and he knew it was coming. Or did he? At one level, of course, he knew in the same way that Fr Rutilio, Archbishop Romero, Ita, Carla and Jean all knew that they were so deeply at risk that, one day, they must surely lose their liberty. Nevertheless, when it happens it's always a shock. It's a shock in the same way that discovering one is HIV positive or has cancer is a shock, a shock that leaves one stunned with the heart racing and the legs turned to jelly.

We don't often think of Jesus with his legs turned to jelly – or any hero, for that matter. It doesn't quite fit with our idea of what it means to be brave. It's a pity, that, because bravery is about living with fear, not about being spared it. The brave know fear all right, deep in their turbulent guts and thudding hearts. The only difference is that they are somehow given the grace to transcend it, to walk when they feel they can't and to talk when their tongue cleaves to their palate. People are amazingly brave. They sing songs, make jokes, write poems in prison, or sit in their hospital rooms holding court like kings for those who are free to walk away. It's only when the bell goes and the last visitor has escaped thankfully into the fresh air that they can remove their brave smiles like grease-paint and lie back wearily on their pillows to reflect upon their powerlessness.

> Man's life is a prison;
> he is sentenced to pain and grief.
> Like a slave he pants for the shadows,
> like a servant he longs for rest.
> Each day I live seems endless,
> and I suffer through endless nights.
> When I lie down, I long for morning,
> When I get up, I long for evening;
> all day I toss and turn.
> My flesh crawls with maggots;
> my skin cracks and oozes.
> My days fly past me like a stubble,
> and my hope snaps like a thread.
>
> Job 7:1–6

We are all terrified of arrest, of loss of liberty, of powerlessness and yet, paradoxically, it can be a time of incredible grace. As I said at the beginning of this chapter, arrest is a watershed, an abrupt transition from one state of life to another. It is the change from the status of free citizen to that of captive, from healthy person to patient, from wife to widow. Arrest is terrible, like birth, that painful, messy emergence from the warmth and security of the womb. It has no beauty or significance in itself, just as death is quite simply a transition, a passing from one world into the next.

Spectators have a tendency to romanticize these moments of passage, ignoring the pain and mess that overwhelm the participants. I get very bored with those who seek to glorify the process of dying, sanitizing it as the most important psychological *experience* of a person's life. Most people are unconscious when they die, or are violently smashed into oblivion by strokes, heart attacks or trauma. They are bundled unceremoniously through the cabin door without so much as a meaningful last word or a farewell kiss until they find themselves falling, falling, falling . . . and then, we believe, the parachute opens . . .

The importance of arrest, like the importance of dying, is what lies beyond the door, the new world into which we are catapulted. The prisoner has much in common with the seriously ill, so I hold them loosely together. Theirs is a stripped pine world, bare like a Carmelite's cell, with its bed, chair, high barred window and just enough food to keep alive. Gone are the easy chairs, the television, novels, chocolates, gone the carpets, curtains, pictures, ornaments, all the things we need to be content. Gone too is our sense of invulnerability, our sleepwalker's certainty that we are masters of the world, that we are in control.

Powerlessness is a sacrament, an outward sign of an inward truth, that we are 'created, sojourners in a land we did not make' (Annie Dillard, *Holy the Firm*), that we are totally and utterly dependent upon the God who made us. Ah, what wisdom, but learned at what cost.

I had thought to illustrate this wisdom of the desert with the writing of some articulate prisoner or terminally ill patient, but perhaps it's more honest to take an ordinary situation; one with which we more readily identify. I say this because although the wisdom of the powerless is commonplace it is not always immediately obvious, being either hidden beneath their surface or expressed in such ordinary language or behaviour that we fail to recognize it: like the disciples on the road to Emmaus, we look for something so different, so impressive, so overtly religious that we are blind to the presence of the Lord in our midst.

Let me, then, tell you Suzi's story, and how her very weakness became an instrument of revelation for those around her.

Suzi was a dancer, an American, a wild, quixotic, exuberant woman who ran a tumbling school for young dancers with her girlfriend Laurie. In 1982 she met an Australian, Vince Lovegrove, on a plane trip and they fell in love. They lived together, as people do, and in June 1985, their son Troy was born. A year later, they were married and, shortly after, their whole world crashed in because Suzi discovered she had AIDS. This was Suzi's moment of 'arrest': 'One minute I was rushing about with the baby and, the next week, there we were, falling downstairs.' Suzi was terrified, not just for herself but for those she loved: 'My mind went like a steam train. I thought, well, I've killed my baby, I've killed my husband, his daughter. Anybody in my house is contaminated.'

By some miracle, Vince was clear, but Troy, the love child of this second marriage, was also affected, so Vince had to face not only Suzi's death but inevitably Troy's as well. Asked how she felt when she found that her child had been contaminated in her womb, Suzi's voice wavered: 'Did you ever want to turn out all the lights and just pull the covers over your head and not come out ever again? You just feel you want to die.'

Sometimes people with AIDS have long remissions during which they remain well, but this was not to be for Suzi. By the end of 1986 she was going downhill fast and the virus had clearly affected her brain, causing severe impairment of her speech and co-ordination. With characteristic humour she described herself: 'I shake, rattle and roll, I shake unbelievably. I know it's my brain . . . It's really doing quite a job . . . I can't do a thing about it.'

In some ways, AIDS is like cancer: a fatal disease, a pillaging army, marching inexorably on, raping and stealing at will. But there is another dimension which puts it into quite a different league of suffering: the social ostracism by friends and neighbours. Vince and Suzi found this particularly difficult to bear. People they had thought of as friends somehow vanished, leaving them to cope as best they could.

> There is cold fear in a time of tribulation,
> a time of the olive press, the wine press,
> the crushing grapes,
> and no guarantee of a good vintage . . .
>
> Jim Cotter *Healing – more or less*

This fear of AIDS is something we have all to come to terms with, for by being afraid, of contagion, of judgement, of our own death we ostracize those who most need our help.

Poor Suzi: her very disability was the prison which contained her, walled in by those who had abandoned her because they now felt ill at ease in her company.

People respond to suffering in many different ways. Had Suzi been a woman of smaller, meaner spirit she might have coped very differently with her illness, becoming introspective and demanding. Vince, too, might have behaved quite differently, finding it impossible to cope with the care of a sick wife and nineteen-month-old baby son. But Suzi and Vince were gifted with a special courage, with a love that demanded to be shared, not buried and gloated upon in secret.

Saddened and angered by the way their friends had treated them they were determined to go public, to make a television film that shared their experience with anyone who would listen, so that more people would understand about the unmentionable experience of having AIDS.

It takes courage to admit to all the world that you've got AIDS, to expose your children to ostracism at school, to risk personal violence. It takes courage, too, to submit to intimate questioning about facing death and to be filmed ill and disabled, asleep or in tears. Suzi and Vince's courage was rewarded for theirs is a most remarkable film, capturing moments of joy and despair, friendship and quite ecstatic love.

At the time she was filmed Suzi was already severely disabled, her speech staccato and laboured, her walking like a drunken sailor's. But through this mask of disability we see quite clearly the real Suzi, not the dancer or the sharp-witted irreverent maverick but a young woman completely selfless in her concern, not for herself but for her family. One of the most moving scenes is when she and Vince talk about her death.

> Suzi: Are you going to be all right . . . You know, when . . . I hope he [Troy] keeps you so damn busy you won't have a moment to think. I wish I could say, 'I know how you feel.' But I'm wearing the other shoe. I worry for you.

As I have tried to explain, the meeting with God in the desert of prison or serious illness is often a very hidden thing and we can recognize it more by the way people behave than by what they say.

For someone as severely disabled as Suzi to be worried, not about her own increasing disability and impending death but how her husband will cope, is grace indeed. It is what Bonhoeffer calls costly grace: bought at great price, by courageous acceptance of suffering. The Spirit of God knows no boundaries and he will attend the deathbed of both saint and sinner. He passes through the prison bars to visit priests and terrorists alike, bestowing his largesse wherever he finds a heart open and ready. The great paradox, of course, is that so often, it is only when we have been arrested, searched and stripped and imprisoned that we are sufficiently empty-handed to receive the gift he offers.

Perhaps, like John Donne, we should pray:

Batter my heart, three person'd God; for, you
As yet but knocke, breathe, shine, and seeke to mend;
That I may rise, and stand, o'er throw mee, and bend
Your force, to breake, blowe, burn and make me new.
I, like an usurpt towne, to another due,
Labour to admit you, but Oh, to no end,
Reason your viceroy in mee, mee should defend,
But is captiv'd and proves weake or untrue.
Yet dearely I love you, and would be loved faine,
But am betroth'd unto your enemie:
Divorce mee, untie, or breake that knot againe,
Take mee to you, imprison mee, for I,
Except you enthrall mee, never shall be free,
Nor ever chaste, except you ravish mee.

Divine Meditations 14

10

The Way of Dispossession

Naked I wait Thy love's uplifted stroke!
My harness piece by piece Thou hast hewn from me,
And smitten me to my knee;
I am defenceless utterly.

Francis Thompson *The Hound of Heaven*

In the summer of 1976, the year after I was released from prison, I spent two weeks at Stanbrook Abbey, a Benedictine monastery for women. The then Lady Abbess, a tall imposing lady not given to pussyfooting, said to me abruptly: 'I knew they'd strip you. They always do.'

At the time, I was somewhat taken aback and found her comment strange – a little intrusive, but over years I have come to understand what she was getting at.

In the traditional Stations of the Cross we have the scene where Jesus is stripped of his garments prior to being scourged. We see him depicted in pious art, a sad, pale figure clad modestly in loincloth or towel, standing humbly before his captors, not unlike the demonstration photographs of patients in medical textbooks, stripped to display the signs of their disease.

But the stripping that happens as an aid to interrogation is not quite like that. There is no loincloth to protect the modesty but a violent insistence on total nakedness so that vulnerability is maximized. Those who work with victims of torture speak of the deliberate perversion of the relationship of intimacy. It is no accident that people are stripped naked, that they are genitally abused, humiliated and raped, for this constitutes the greatest humiliation that one human being can inflict upon another.

And yet, it is possible, after a while to transcend the shame of vulnerability, to regain an equilibrium and inner certainty that one's personhood and dignity lie beyond mere externals and are therefore unassailable. We see this triumph of the spirit over brutality most clearly in prison literature, particularly the poetry.

When they want
us to keep being a number
without a soul, destroyed –
they forget
that though everything
may be lost on the way:
homes, goods, so many broken ties
they forget
that the Chilean
is made of oak and luma
never bent by storm.
They forget
that in the sky
there is an indestructible star
our star
which will be
always
our goal, our course and our guide.

Anon. Tres Alamos Detention Camp,
Chile 1975

This song written in Tres Alamos prison where I spent two months in 1975 is echoed in Irina Ratushinskaya's more sophisticated poem, written in prison eight years later in November 1983.

I will live and survive and be asked:
How they slammed my head against a trestle,
How I had to freeze at nights
How my hair started to turn grey . . .
And I'll smile – And will crack some joke
And brush away the encroaching shadow.
And I will render homage to the dry September
That became my second birth.
And I'll be asked: 'Doesn't it hurt you to remember?'
Not being deceived by my outward flippancy.

But the former names will detonate in my memory –
Magnificent as old cannon.
And I will tell of the best people in all the earth,
The most tender, but also the most invincible,
How they said farewell, how they went to be tortured,
How they waited for letters from their loved ones.
Irina Ratushinskaya

Just as powerlessness reminds us that we are sojourners in our world, nakedness reminds us of what it means to be a person. It tells us of our common humanity, our beauty and vulnerability as living, loving, thinking, sexual beings. More than anything it reminds us that we are body, mind and spirit and that we ignore any one of these three sides of our nature at our peril.

And yet, ignore them we do. When our bodies are young and strong and beautiful we are full of a delicious animal vigour. The sap races in our veins and, exulting in our humanity, we are tempted to spurn ideas of the world of the spirit as childish fantasy or old wives' tales. We work and play, eat and sleep, love and hate as if we would live for ever, blind as moles to the reality of the world beyond our horizon.

Then, for some of us, reality breaks through and we are blinded by a dazzling darkness, by the spiritual dimension of our existence. This encounter with the transcendent is not an intellectual event. We do not study theology and suddenly know that there is a God and that we should worship him, although that *can* happen. It is much more in the nature of things, however, that we meet God in the desert, in sickness, prison, bereavement or some other desolation. As the philosopher puts it, 'Pain is a holy angel which shows treasure to men which otherwise remains forever hidden' (Adalbert Stiffer). Stiffer's Holy Angel is echoed again and again in the writings of the poets and mystics, men like the fourteenth-century Rhineland mystic Meister Eckhart: 'The faithful God often lets his friends fall sick and lets every prop on which they lean be knocked out from under them.' True, we say, in fact, too true to be funny. It happened to Job. It happens all the time. Why? 'Listen', says Eckhart. 'It is a great joy to loving people to be able to do important things such as watching, fasting and the like, beside sundry more different undertakings.'

Sure, we say: that and a lot more. Caring for the sick, running a parish, teaching little children. Of course we enjoy doing our good works – the Lord's work. Wait, says Eckhart: here's the catch.

> In such things they find their joy, their stay and hope. Thus their pious works are supports, stays or footings to them. [*This* is the reason why the Lord takes these things away.] Our Lord wants his friends to be rid of such notions. That is why he removes every prop, so that he alone may support them . . . For the more helpless and destitute the mind that turns to God for support can be, the deepest the person penetrates God and the more sensitive he is to God's most valuable gifts. Man must build on God alone.
>
> Meister Eckhart
> *Talks of Instruction No. 10*

So there we have it. Eckhart clearly sees the hand of God in suffering, believing that God in stripping people of their supports reveals to them not only their utter dependence upon him but his overwhelming love for them.

What a theory! True or false? How can we know? Here we are plunged up to our eyeballs in the mystery of suffering. I do not know the answer but I feel very comfortable with Eckhart's theory, as I do with Job's awe-filled answer to God:

> I know that you are all-powerful:
> what you conceive, you can perform.
> I am the man who obscured your designs
> with my empty-headed words.
> I have been holding forth on matters I cannot understand,
> on marvels beyond me and my knowledge . . .
> I knew you then only by hearsay;
> but now, having seen you with my own eyes,
> I retract all I have said,
> and in dust and ashes I repent.[1]

'Having seen you with my own eyes . . . ' Herein lies the key to Job's acquiescence and to ours. Like Jacob, he has wrestled with the stranger and been wounded. He has *met* God, in struggle and darkness, and finds he has 'carnal' knowledge of him, i.e. his knowledge of God has moved from his intellect to his heart or, if you prefer it, to his guts.

The Job story is an archetype of suffering humankind's relationship with God and perhaps can only be fully understood by those who have experienced the stripping of powerlessness. For them the message is very clear. Suffering is devastating, one would never wish for it, but in some mysterious way it can be the occasion of an encounter with God which is both terrifying and supremely wonderful, for God is love and his love is 'better than life itself'.[2]

There is a very real danger that, in trying to wrest a spiritual meaning from suffering, we get lured into glorifying it and thereby denying its awfulness. I myself did this for a number of years by trying to over-spiritualize my experience of torture. So convinced was I of my encounter with God in prison that I denied to myself and everyone else what a devastating experience it had been. It was only when, many years later, I had to cope with the psychological aftermath of the experience – what is called the post traumatic stress syndrome – that I was able to acknowledge how wounded I had been. This admission in no way negated the spiritual dimension of the experience: it was indeed a very precious time of closeness to God – but it was also very terrible indeed. Such understanding as I have of my own experience confirms for me how important it is for us to maintain a paschal overview of suffering, holding in the same focus the awful reality of suffering and the mind-blowing truth that God is somehow in it.

Perhaps it's important, then, that we should not always keep a stiff upper lip, not always make light of our pain. I find that I value more and more the honesty of men like Father Jimmy Doherty who have the courage not only to battle with their pain but to admit publicly to their depression and their tears.

Jimmy Doherty is an Irish Roman Catholic priest who after his ordination in 1967 went to work in Derry in the North of Ireland. He threw himself cheerfully into parish work, learning to love and respect the people with whom he worked.

> I marvelled at the inner strength of ordinary people who survived well despite many disadvantages . . . large families

> being able to live in cramped flats, men on the dole taking care of their children while their wives spent long arduous hours in shirt factories; men and women giving long hours to voluntary community work, helping others to cope with poverty, sickness and various tragic situations.[3]

It's curious how those whose lives are caught up in helping others somehow think of themselves as immune from the troubles that befall their clients. Doctors and nurses are as indignant as the next man or woman when their bodies fail them and social workers are taken unawares when their spouses are unfaithful. The world, alas, is not divided into carers and clients but we must all take our turn playing different roles. Jimmy's turn to play 'patient' came very early on for in his first year as a priest he had a number of peculiar attacks of weakness which landed him briefly in hospital for investigations. Perhaps if he had wanted to know the truth the doctors would have told him that he might have Multiple Sclerosis – but he chose to ignore his symptoms and carry on with his life. At first this policy seemed to pay off for the attacks disappeared and he was able to involve himself ever more deeply in his ministry. It was 1972 and the beginning of 'the troubles', and this description of 'Bloody Sunday' makes chilling reading.

> As I was on hospital duty that evening I decided to go to Altragelvin Hospital and give what assistance I could. My memory of the visit to the hospital morgue will remain with me for the rest of my life. Bodies were being brought in and laid on the ground surface of the morgue, each body being covered with a sheet. Not knowing who had or had not been anointed, I proceeded to anoint each body as it lay prone and stiff on the floor. It was an eerie experience as policemen and army personnel were in constant attention. For the next number of hours, I met relatives and friends who had come to identify the bodies. Their constant screaming and crying penetrated my brain and my heart. I stayed at the hospital until midnight and eventually made my way back to the parochial house and went to bed as if in a daze.[4]

As the troubles continued, Jimmy Doherty's life became

more and more closely entwined with those of his people. Just a year later he was again confronted with tragedy when a public house in his parish was attacked by gunmen.

> Again I was on duty and when I reached the public house, an angry crowd was gathering outside. Once again I spent sometime walking over dead bodies with blood splashed on the floor. This was the first extreme act of 'sectarianism' within our parish, but by this time my innermost desire was to heal community division rather than seek revenge.[5]

Spurred on by this bloody killing, Jimmy joined forces with a Presbyterian minister and together they began to work for reconciliation between their people.

I was in Chile during these early years of 'the troubles' and Jimmy Doherty's accounts of his ministry took me by surprise. I suppose I knew in the head but not in the heart what it was like to live in Derry at that time, 'almost once a month for several years, I found myself on the streets trying to calm angry teenagers and to separate warring factions.' As a community pastor he was caught up many times in the people's conflict. Once it was to seek the release of a Catholic man held captive on a Protestant estate, he went with the army captain into the Protestant stronghold:

> We arrived at the estate within ten minutes to see a line of masked men blocking off the entrance to the estate. The captain and I got out of the jeep and walked towards the line. Each masked man had a cudgel which he beat on the ground in perfect timing to the walk of the captain and myself. I felt a cold sweat break out on my back.[6]

Eventually the man was released, scared and shocked by his ordeal (he had been burnt by cigarette ends). Before the night was out a Protestant man had been kidnapped in retaliation and Jimmy was drawn in once more.

There were other episodes: one night he was detained and roughly handled by the police.

> I was very conscious that no one else was in sight and when we came to the police station, he advised me that I lean on the wall with my arms to support me and to keep

> my legs wide apart. He reached over me, took my licence and called to another soldier who was told to check out my identity. I stood there in a rather uncomfortable posture. I could feel the rifle pressed against my back. I was held for about three or four minutes. It seemed much longer.[7]

Another night, he took the place of one of his parishioners who had been 'ordered' by the IRA to meet them in one of the 'no-go areas'.

Perhaps if he'd led a quieter more 'traditional' priestly life Jimmy Doherty's M.S. would not have returned; but he didn't and it did. 'Then came the rare sensation of pins and needles in my legs. These came and went during the day but returned more forcibly each night. And I began to feel more and more tired.'

Conscious that he was risking both emotional and spiritual burnout, Jimmy formed a 'fraternity' with some of his brother priests and met each month to pray, reflect and have fun together. He found the support group enormously helpful and, as he tried to pray more regularly, his life of the spirit deepened.

Lay people are often tempted to believe that priests and nuns have some kind of hot line to God but they too have to discipline themselves to pray.

One of Jimmy's thirteen-year-old parishioners summed up his condition when she said, 'You're so busy being a busy priest that you're too busy.' Gradually, however, he learned to be still and to wait upon God in silence. Sometimes his prayer was sweet and he was conscious of God's presence, but just as often he felt nothing and had to struggle with darkness and disbelief. In hindsight, he sees this period as a preparation for the suffering that was to come: 'It may be easy to conjecture that in some unknown and silent way I was being prepared to learn the meaning of weakness, the meaning of being dependent, of being out of control so that someone greater would be in control.'[8]

During this period of learning to walk in faith, his physical health was deteriorating. The pins and needles and the fatigue continued but he continued to ignore them. In hindsight he sees this as unconscious denial because of a terror that his priestly life and, therefore, his whole sense of identity was threatened.

> A deeply committed priest justifies his being by the hours of dedicated slogging which he can clock up . . . In some sense the attacks on my body were mere distractions from my work and at worst were frustrating moments in my fast living. My need to be busy and involved contributed a lot to my denial of sickness and my refusal to take it seriously. If I were to take it seriously, it might interfere with my priesthood.[9]

The day came, however, when he was forced to acknowledge what was happening and seek medical advice. His moment of 'arrest' had come. It happened while he was shaving.

> Suddenly my arms fell by my side and refused to move. I stumbled back to my bed trying to blow the soap suds from my mouth and eyes and the only thing I could do was sit there. Within two minutes, power was restored to my arms and I washed the suds from my face, dried myself and stood looking at myself in the mirror. 'My God,' I whispered. 'What is going wrong?'

Still he didn't go to the doctor, ignoring a number of similar episodes until, one night while producing a play at the local community centre, he fell off the stage onto a row of chairs. At last, his denial was challenged and he agreed to go to the hospital for tests.

Two weeks in the local hospital were followed by four weeks at the Royal Victoria Hospital in Belfast, but still no diagnosis was forthcoming. Surrounded by very sick men in the neurology ward, he faced the possibilities. 'Frightening thoughts passed through my mind. – "I have a tumour, I have six months to live." "An operation would be pointless."'

Eventually, however, his turn came and he was told that the doctor would see him.

> So I put on my best priestly face to hear the bad news. I braced myself and waited and when the young doctor said my sickness had no name, I felt disappointed, even cheated. It was compared to an electrical short in my system which

> caused the brain messages to be disrupted and I was assured that it would not cause me any serious damage. And so I was told I could go home.

Did they not know, I wonder? Or did the doctors think that 'M.S.' was too cruel a diagnosis? Perhaps they thought it was kinder to lie.

Lies can be very comforting – for a while. The trouble is, most people aren't deceived for long. Jimmy Doherty was no exception. Eventually, he decided to come to London to seek a second opinion. This time the doctor was straight with him.

> He looked at me with calmness and firmness and asked, 'Do you want to know?' 'Yes please', I said . . . 'You have Multiple Sclerosis, albeit a benign form', he replied. I sat calmly listening to him as he explained what that meant, assuring me that the possibility of my being in a wheelchair was very remote – that he would write to my neurologist in Belfast. His words faded away into nothingness, as my insides began to crumble. In my mind I was screaming, Oh no, not me, not that, please God, no, no, no. My screaming came from the awful frightening possibility of having to depend upon a wheelchair for mobility.

Terrified, Jimmy at last faced his own mortality head on, and with it the possibility that his busy priesthood, 'my work ethic syndrome', might be completely lost. With that loss he faced, as all people with serious illness eventually must, the loss of his own sense of personal worth. 'After all, what worth would I have if I could not visit schools, visit homes, spend long hours counselling and helping people – what value would I have? – this just could not be true.'

Jimmy returned to his parish but the months that followed were difficult, 'full of turmoil, despair, depression, new beginnings, determination, weakness and courage.' Gradually, he learned to live with his illness, letting go of some of his work and resting for a couple of hours in the afternoon. It was a time of darkness and he was shocked one day to find himself thinking about suicide. 'I rolled the bottle between my thumb and finger and remember that the thought raced through my mind, "one big swallow and it will all be over."'[10]

In 1982 Jimmy Doherty resigned his post as pastor of

Creggan parish and moved to a much smaller country parish. The move cost him dear, 'with my heart breaking into small fragments', as he said goodbye forever, not just to the parish that he loved but to a style of ministry in which he was an integral part of the community.

Just one week after the move, his mother died and he was overwhelmed by her loss.

> Her death cut into me deeply as I collapsed in a heap onto the floor. Again it was some years later before I fully realized the grieving that swept over me – the grieving of these deaths, my mother's, my health, and my parish. The pain went deep and somehow in some strange way the three grievings were not clearly separated or defined. That added to the darkness and confusion and erupted into an internal scream to God, 'What more do you want? Where are you taking me now? Why? Why? Oh why?'

The new parish did not really work out and in 1984, Jimmy moved again, this time to be a school chaplain. Here at least, he could manage the work and began to be involved in working with people with M.S. and other handicaps. Externally he seemed to be coping well, but,

> Deep inside I was in knots. Emotionally this was expressed in outbursts of temper, of quietly shedding tears. During one of these periods I had a very touching experience. One afternoon as I sat in my room, ruminating about priesthood, missing the privilege and opportunity of saying mass with people, the tears filled my eyes and ran down my face. At that moment my housekeeper, Mary, entered, saw the state in which I was, knelt at my feet, looked up at my face and gently whispered, 'M. . . . S. – Messy Stuff.'

That sums it up really. Stripping, whether by violence, illness or bereavement, is a messy business. We look at the heroes, the brave survivors and are deceived by their outer serenity. Ignorant of their tears and rage, we forget that there is no shortcut to freedom, that:

> In order to arrive there,
> To arrive where you are, to get from where you are not,
> You must go by a way wherein there is no ecstasy.

In order to arrive at what you do not know
You must go by a way which is the way of ignorance.
In order to possess what you do not possess
You must go by the way of dispossession.
T. S. Eliot 'East Coker', *Four Quartets*

Lord, we are afraid,
we are afraid of you,
of what you may ask.
We yearn for your coming,
for your love, for your passion,
but we are afraid.
We cling to the familiar,
to people and things,
terrified of trading
the security of the known,
for a future beyond imagining.
Give us your courage
to say 'Yes'.

11

Torture

I did not stain my spirit with hatred,
but I have seen the anguish
and the epileptic terror
of naked men electrocuted.

Speaking with the Children
written in a Chilean prison camp 1974

They didn't have electricity in Jesus' day, so they couldn't use it to torture him. Instead, we're told, they scourged him, whipping his naked body with leather thongs which had little gadgets at the end that tore into his flesh. When they'd had their fill of beating him (or more likely when they decided he couldn't take any more) they put a crown of thorns upon his head, and, dressing him up as a king, taunted and mocked him, bending the knee before him with the salutation, 'Hail, king of the Jews'.

It was a bit like that for Victor, too, when he was softened up for interrogation. One of the army officers, recognizing him as a well-known folk-singer, separated him from the other prisoners, putting him in a special gallery reserved for 'dangerous' or 'important' prisoners. Later in the day, he was spotted by the second-in-command of the Stadium, a tall blonde officer nicknamed 'The Prince'. The meeting was witnessed by another prisoner: 'As Victor came face to face with him, he gave a sign of recognition and smiled sarcastically. Mimicking playing a guitar, he giggled and then quickly drew his finger across his throat.' Riled by Victor's calm he shouted to the guards, 'Don't let him move from here. This one is reserved for me.'[1]

Just what they did to Victor we'll probably never know. He was glimpsed briefly lying on the floor of the basement changing rooms, covered with blood, on a floor awash with filth from an overflowing lavatory. When they had finished with him, they brought him back to join the other prisoners.

> He could scarcely walk, his head and his face were bloody and bruised, one of his ribs seemed to be broken and he was in pain from where he had been kicked in the stomach. His friends wiped his face and tried to make him more comfortable. One of them had a small jar of jam and some biscuits. They shared the food between three or four of them, dipping their fingers into the jam one after the other and licking every vestige of it.[2]

Veronica wipes the face of Jesus. Victor's friends clean up his blood-stained visage. Biscuits and jam, loaves and fishes, Chile or Jerusalem, the whole sad saga continues.

A few weeks ago, I hosted a reception at the hospice to raise money, not for our own cause but for another charity, The Medical Foundation for the Care of Victims of Torture. The Medical Foundation is a very small organization based in London, which provides medical, social and psychological care for men, women and children who have been tortured. Last year, they treated over a thousand 'cases', men like this one:

'A young man arrived in London after a complicated series of moves between various countries, and was living with family friends. He had been held in prison for some three years after his initial period of arrest and torture . . . On being arrested, he was blindfolded, taken to a building where the blindfold was removed and he was locked in a cell where he found a friend who had four toes cut off. He was later taken down some stairs to a small room, measuring approximately two metres by two metres. It was covered with blood. There was a lot of broken glass and broken bottles on the floor. There were three people present in the room, whom he feels he would recognize again. They wore no uniform. He was stripped naked; his hands and feet were bound and he was hung upside down from a bar on the ceiling with a rope around his feet. The torturers beat him with a wire cable, mainly to the legs and soles of his feet, and cut him on the soles of his feet with glass pieces. They burnt him with lighted cigarettes applied between the fingers and on the backs of the hands. Periodically, a blood-stained blanket was stuffed into his mouth to prevent his cries. On several occasions the guards passed urine into his mouth. At a later point he was hung up again, punched in the mouth and he estimates that six of his teeth were broken. One of the interrogators pulled several of these broken teeth with a pair of pliers. Twenty-four hours later he was subject to a mock execution. Together with five other prisoners, he was tied to a pole, blindfolded, and when the shots rang out he alone was alive. He was then locked up with the five corpses and left with them for some time. On two occasions he was bled, approximately three hundred c.c. of blood being taken from a vein. He knew that other people had been executed in this manner, simply by the draining of blood until they died.'

I have quoted this cruel description in its entirety because, I believe, we need sometimes to share in the pain of those who have been tortured. The psychotherapist, from whose report I have taken this description, speaks of the people in his group, all of whom have been through experiences comparable to the one described above. There were seven patients in his therapy group: three from the Middle East, two from Africa, one from South East Asia and one from South America. One of the 'clients', the South American, told the group that, 'until he met us he did not find anybody who could encompass the terms of his anguish. And so, he told us, "the forest was my doctor". The forest alone, a patch of beech wood near his family home in a county near London, was a place to which he went when he cried, shouted and ran about in great distress in periods of anguish, relieving his pent-up emotions and discovering that the forest could encompass what no person individually had yet been able to do.'

The Medical Foundation was formed in an attempt to encompass such grief, to form a container for the sea of tears of the tortured. They used to have their base at a London hospital, but this year they were evicted to make room for more administration. Now they are desperately raising money for new premises – hence these meetings.

After the reception at the hospice, we moved on to the hospital for another meeting, this time restricted to medical people. One of the doctors from the Foundation had come down to talk about his work and I was to speak briefly about my own experience. We had circulated five hundred doctors, and naively, I expected a big turn-out, perhaps sixty or more. I suppose, if I'd thought it through, I'd have realized people might be reluctant: after all, it's a distasteful subject and no one likes turning out at night for lectures. We walked into the auditorium and surveyed the audience: all ten of them, huddled sheepishly in the centre of the room. I nearly wept; I just couldn't believe that my colleagues would not be interested to hear a fellow doctor – a surgeon – talk about such work.

At an *intellectual* level, of course, I understand. I know all too well about compassion fatigue and I know that I don't turn out to hear about other people's charities. But somehow, I'd thought, this one was different.

I think it's my fury and impotence at the widespread use of torture that has, more than anything, fired me to write this book. On the one hand, we read the endless obscene descriptions of cruelty that emerge from countries where torture is practised, facts that no one, myself included, wants to know about. 'Humankind,' as Eliot reminds us, 'cannot bear too much reality.' On the other hand, we dwell upon the passion story, dramatizing it in art and music, weeping over the 'Sacred Head ill used by reed and bramble scarred'. 'Were you there when they crucified my Lord?', the singer croons and the music makes my heart burst. No, I want to scream, no, I wasn't there – but I *was* there in Chile, when they tortured some poor bastard in the next room, and I heard his screams with my own ears. I was there too when the guard threw his blood-stained shirt at us to wash and I have sat hour after hour at a Finnish Tribunal listening to the revolting evidence of humankind's inhumanity.

What *should* we do about torture, I ask myself, and I don't really know the answer. I just know that we need to take the tears we shed for Jesus and use them to wash the blood-stained faces of the Good Friday people of our own day. We need to harness our grief and anger at the way Jesus suffered to try and end the suffering of our own people. What is wrong with our society that an organization like the Medical Foundation is evicted from its premises so that it has to pay someone to raise enough money to buy a house where the victims of torture can be treated? We should be insisting that such people receive the best care that medical science can offer, that no expense be spared in the attempt to make restitution for the wrongs that they have suffered.

> We should be in mourning,
> we should be in tears,
> our blinds should be perpetually drawn.
>
> John Harriott *Our World*

Lord, we sit
in sackcloth and ashes.
We are a poor people,
weak and wounded,
soiled and guilty.
We know we are trapped
in the sin of our world,
by torture and rape,
hunger and child abuse.
Lord, we cry out,
from the depths of our pain:
Rend the heavens
and come down,
pull us out of the mire,
for we are going under.

12

Crucify Him, Crucify Him

The Governor was strong upon
The Regulations Act.
The Doctor said that Death was but
A scientific fact:
And twice a day the Chaplain called,
And left a little tract.

Oscar Wilde
The Ballad of Reading Gaol

When the torturers had finished with Jesus, Pilate presented him to the crowd, thinking they would be appeased by seeing him so hurt and humiliated – but they were not to be moved, and shouted with one voice, 'Crucify him! Crucify him'. And Pilate who was a weak man, and afraid of trouble, did the expedient thing, and sentenced Jesus to death.

There is something obscene about the death penalty: something much worse than all the terrible things that people do to each other in anger or for lust, for gain or for revenge. Oscar Wilde captures the feel of this in *The Ballad of Reading Gaol* in which he writes of a prisoner awaiting execution for killing his mistress.

I never saw a man who looked
With such a wistful eye
Upon that little tent of blue
Which prisoners call the sky,
And at every drifting cloud that went
With sails of silver by.

I walked, with other souls in pain,
Within another ring,

And was wondering if the man had done
A great or little thing,
When a voice behind me whispered low,
'That fellow's got to swing.'

Dear Christ, the very prison walls
Suddenly seemed to reel,
And the sky above my head became
Like a casque of scorching steel;
And, though I was a soul in pain,
My pain I could not feel.

I only knew what hunted thought
Quickened his step, and why
He looked upon the garish day
With such a wistful eye;
The man had killed the thing he loved,
And so he had to die.

It's not just that by condemning a person to death we inflict upon them the agony of all who know that they must die, but that we do it in the name of justice. I find it somehow blasphemous that we take upon ourselves the right to end the life of another human being. I know that lives are taken every day by murderers, terrorists, the secret police: but somehow that is different. They are sick, or wicked, or driven, but we, we do it in cold blood, in public, in the name of God. When I say *we* do it, of course I don't mean we in England, because we no longer practise the death penalty. But there are many nations which do, and there are people in this country who call for its return.

Jesus of Nazareth was condemned to death, because Pilate, a weak man, was anxious to appease the Jews. It's easy to see how it happened. The chief priests had been out to get Jesus for a long time because everything he said and did posed a threat to the whited sepulchre of a church that they had built for themselves. Now, it seemed, he had played right into their hands with his blasphemous talk of destroying the Temple. Carefully the high priest posed his question, laying it like a net at Jesus' feet. 'Are you the Christ,' he said, 'the son of the Blessed One?'

And Jesus stepped right into it: 'I am,' he said, 'and you will see the Son of Man seated at the right hand of the Power and coming with the clouds of heaven.' The high priest was ecstatic. The fool had fallen right into his trap; they'd got him, at last. He tore his robes in a histrionic exhibition of dismay. 'What need of witnesses have we now?' he crowed.[1] 'You've heard the blasphemy. What is your finding?' And the jury was unanimous. The lawyer and the shop girl, the respectable married woman and the doctor all nodded their heads and agreed that the prisoner had condemned himself out of his own mouth. They were very sorry, but they had no option but to find him guilty. 'And they all gave their verdict: he deserved to die.'

And there and then, they turned on him. The very people who less than a week ago had acclaimed him as a hero began to spit on him, hurling abuse as he ran the gauntlet of the crowd, a pitiful figure only partly hidden by the blanket pulled over his face. The lights flashed and the TV cameras rolled as he stumbled down the court-house steps and was guided blindly towards the safety of the waiting police car.

How did he feel, I wonder? Like the foolish drug smuggling teenager in Bangkok, or like Fazard Bazoft, the journalist sentenced to die for spying in Baghdad?

> In Debtor's Yard the stones are hard,
> And the dripping wall is high,
> So there it was he took the air
> Beneath a leaden sky,
> And by each side a warden walked,
> For fear the man might die.
>
> Or else he sat with those who watched
> His anguish night and day;
> Who watched him when he rose to weep,
> And when he crouched to pray;
> Who watched him lest himself should rob
> Their scaffold of its prey.
>
> Oscar Wilde
> *The Ballad of Reading Gaol*

Facing death is never easy, not even for the very old who know that their time is running out. For the young it is unbearably hard, cut off as they are in the springtime of their lives, before they can bear fruit. It was like that for Jenny when I sat beside her bed last night looking at her pale pinched little face and told her that we could not cure her cancer. She stared at me in disbelief. This couldn't be happening to *her*. It couldn't be true. At last the tears ran down her face and she gulped, 'It isn't fair', and I said, 'No – it isn't fair. I'm sorry. I wish I could magic it all away, but I can't. I'm not God. I'm only a doctor, and sometimes we can't make people better.'

Oh it was hard. Hard for her and hard for me to sit there impotently while this twenty-six year old wrestled with such appalling knowledge and then plucked up the courage to ask me how long she'd got. I sat there squirming, wishing I was out on the river, at home, anywhere else but there, beside her bed. What should I say? Should I lie? Was it too hard to tell her I thought she probably had about a month but maybe it was much less? What did *she* think, I wondered. Did she think it was years? So many people do. They simply can't understand that the body in which they live is betraying them, that it is being destroyed minute by minute as they sit there waiting for an answer to their question . . .

Now, twenty-four hours later, the phone rings and the nurse tells me that Jenny has put on her lipstick and is asking to go home. Perhaps we should have told her last week or the week before . . . but she didn't ask and it seemed too cruel to just march in and tell her. You see, telling someone they are going to die is almost like passing sentence on them yourself. It's no wonder doctors often can't find the courage to do it.

Hard as it is for Jenny it was harder still for Suzi. Jenny's dying of cancer, a nice 'respectable' disease. Everyone loves her and is trying desperately to make things easier for her. No one can take away the fear and the sense of loss but at least she knows she is loved. But for Suzi, things are different, because AIDS is definitely not a socially acceptable disease, even if you got it from a blood transfusion, from 'normal' sexual contact, or from your own mother. So Suzi stands doubly condemned: sentenced to death by her disease and sentenced to fear and alienation from the community in which she lives.

The AIDS situation is a scandal of our time – a scandal not because, as some people believe, God is punishing his people for their wanton promiscuity but because so many people are condemning their suffering brothers and sisters in the name of God.

What happens to us Christian people when we distort the gospel message? Wherever did we get the idea that God has called us to sit in judgement on each other? Have we forgotten the story of the woman taken in adultery, dragged naked from her lover's bed and hauled in front of the synod, the mothers' union or the parish council? Weeping, she stands there, her mascara running all over the place, clutching the sheet to her bosom while we, the Sanhedrin, the jury, sit in self-righteous judgement. She is promiscuous, she is depraved, she is dirty, she is gay; she is unnatural, a whore, a disgrace. She is a princess to be executed, a prostitute to be examined for V.D., a gay to be sacked, thrown out of the house with her furniture piled ignominiously on the pavement.

But wait, what was it Jesus said? Perhaps he spoke so low we didn't catch his words; but someone heard it and wrote it down for posterity. 'Let him who is without sin cast the first stone.' And then, as we shuffled in our shoes, and looked this way and that he said to the woman: 'Does no one condemn you? Then neither do I. Go, and sin no more.'[2]

'Go, and sin no more.' 'I say, forgive your brother, not seven times, but seventy times seven.' *That* is what Jesus said. It comes over again and again. 'What I want is mercy not sacrifice' and 'judge not that you may not be judged.' And yet, judge we do, and we mock the social workers who try to explain a man's sin by talking about his deprived childhood.

When I was a teenager at school they taught us to say three Hail Marys each night for 'purity'. Now, in my middle years, it seems much more important to pray for a merciful heart so that I can welcome the wounded and the sinner the way that Jesus would welcome them.

What is it, I wonder, that makes us so ready to judge instead of to forgive? Perhaps it's fear – fear of what people will do to us and fear that our own frailty will be found out. It is said that the most violent homophobes are those who are unsure of their own sexuality and are afraid deep down that they themselves are homosexual.

I find the present climate of intolerance of gay men and women very sad. Perhaps it is inevitable because people are so afraid of contracting AIDS and fear so often turns to hate. My heart aches for those who must face not only their own impending death but the possibility of rejection by their family or religious community. Just when they should be protected and sustained by the love and understanding of those close to them they must live a life of exhausting subterfuge, pretending that all is well or that they have some other disease. I sometimes wonder if it's better to be dying of AIDS in Africa than in England because at least they are not caught up in the crippling tangle of lies.

This sad mess of condemnation and rejection is not confined to the AIDS scene. How quick we are to pounce on another's weakness and forget whatever good has gone before. When a man or woman falls from grace, their misdemeanours are proclaimed from the house-tops, but people rarely ask 'How is John (or Mary) now?' How does it feel to be in his or her shoes? Is his heart broken, her life destroyed? It seems to me that whether the accusations against a person are true or false, it matters how they are. What matters is not that they should be tried and pilloried but they should have friends with whom they can weep and rage as they struggle to rebuild their lives.

In the book of the prophet Ezekiel, God tells his people that he will take away their heart of stone and give to them a heart of flesh. How much more important it seems to me that we should have a vulnerable loving heart of flesh rather than one which is so stony that it has never been tempted. Perhaps Jesus was speaking of this in the parable of the talents.[3] The man who risked his heart, opening it to love, found that it had grown and expanded while the man who locked his in a rust-proof box and buried it for safe keeping found that when the time came to give it back it had shrivelled beyond repair. We forget that prostitutes, tax collectors and sinners are welcome in the Kingdom and that those who have loved much are forgiven much.

What happens, I wonder, to turn people's hearts to stone? I was deeply moved the other night to see a television film about the abandoned children in Rumania. It seems that Ceausescu forbade the use of any kind of birth control and expected each woman to have four or five children. The results of this enforced population explosion were as devastating as they were unexpected: many of the women simply could not cope with their unwanted children and abandoned them. There are now over one hundred thousand unwanted children in Rumania herded together in bleak orphanages, gazing with sad blank eyes into an unknown future.

Appalling as the material plight of these children was, I was struck even more by the lack of loving carers. The paediatrician in charge of the orphanages spoke with deep sadness of the difficulty they had in getting suitable women to care for these babies, many of whom were so disturbed by lack of love that they banged their heads on their cot bars until they bled.

What terrible sickness and apathy have befallen this people that they can lock little children away until they die of starvation – starvation not of food but of love? And what should we be doing to help this people not just rebuild their lives but unfreeze their hearts? How can we rekindle their fire so that they awaken and rise from their tombs to storm the orphanages and carry their children off to a new life?

Holy Spirit of God
Send forth your light and your truth
and enkindle in us the fire of your love.
We beg your comfort for all who face death:
men and women with terminal cancer,
people with AIDS,
prisoners in the condemned cell.
Brand in our hearts the knowledge
that we are called
not to judge, but to forgive.
Give us the power to comfort the frightened

and the faith to know
deep in our hearts
that death is the beginning,
not the end.

13

A Man from the Country

In the bearing of another's burdens,
in the sharing of one another's pain,
we begin to dance.

Jim Cotter
Healing – more or less

When Pilate had done with him, the soldiers led Jesus out of the city and up the hill to Golgotha to execute him. Perhaps he wasn't very strong, or perhaps he was weakened by what they had done to him, but it seems he couldn't manage to carry his cross. Rather than carry it themselves, the soldiers grabbed a passer-by, Simon of Cyrene, 'a man from the country', and made him carry Jesus' cross.

It can't have been much fun for Simon: the cross was heavy and the road was uphill. The bystanders must have wondered who he was: perhaps they thought he was a relative. Perhaps like Jesus, he too was jeered at and spat upon.

I wonder what he thought, deep in his heart? Was he irritated at having his journey interrupted, uncomfortable at being mixed up in someone else's problems, at being so close to such terrible suffering? It must have hurt, too, if he was an ordinary sort of man: you can't go really close to someone in pain without sharing, in some way, in that pain. But pain shared means pain easier to bear, so perhaps he felt good about that: even humbled to have been chosen so unexpectedly to walk alongside this man as he faced his death.

And after it was all over, when he returned to his farm or wherever it was, what effect did it have on his life? Did he forget all about it and carry on, or did he stop, sometimes, as he ploughed his field and think about that quiet man, wonder at all the talk and the stories of peculiar goings-on?

Perhaps it made him more aware of the suffering on his own patch, of the lepers and the cripples, the poor and the outcast. Of course we can only speculate about these things, but it interests me because so many of the people I meet who are involved in caring for the dying were drawn into it, in the first place, quite by accident.

For me, Simon stands as an archetype of the men and women who accompany those in pain. We are all called to share to some extent in the anguish of our fellows, but some people become what Jim Cotter calls 'voluntary pain bearers', absorbing people's anger and pain and caring for them without question and with love. It is important that we look at these 'voluntary pain bearers' for they are often the only source of light in a situation of unspeakable darkness. More than that, they are the conduits by which the love of God is channelled into the arid hearts of those close to despair.

Almost all my Good Friday people are pain bearers – that is why I chose them. I am interested, not in the blackness of their world, the hunger, the war, the sickness or the despair but in the light which they shed. I seek out their light quite instinctively because I know that the light with which they illuminate the world around them is not their own, but God's. They are my ICON PEOPLE, and as I stare into their faces my gaze becomes focussed for depth and I know just a little more of what God is like.

When I say that Simon of Cyrene stands as an archetype of those who accompany the afflicted I do not pretend that he was a particularly holy man: it's most likely that he was very ordinary and that he only shouldered Jesus' cross under duress. But that's the very point I'm trying to illustrate: so often those who find themselves called to bear another's pain are both ordinary and unwilling. In the hospice world we are very wary of taking on staff or volunteers who are too idealistic or too religious. We avoid like the plague those who feel that they are God's gift to the dying. Instead we choose rather ordinary men and women with an earthy practicality and a broad sense of humour: men and women 'from the country'. It is these unselfconscious carers who are able to take our people to their hearts without condition and without expectation. They are able to love the way Jesus loved: unconditionally and unilaterally and, because they are fully human and have other interests, they are able to sustain their caring – are less likely to 'burn out'.

People involved in caring frequently become objects of admiration. They find themselves suddenly hoisted onto the shoulders of the crowd, and carried in triumph towards the nearest pedestal, where they are ceremoniously elevated. It's a pity, that, because heroes should be emulated, not worshipped from afar. More important still, we are all called to be voluntary pain bearers, to share in the burden of caring for each other. There simply are not enough professional carers to visit all the lonely old people in our world and there are nowhere near enough counsellors to support those whose marriages are in difficulty or who are troubled in one way or another. Sharing the pain of those we love and those we trip over on the road to Jerusalem is part of the condition of being human.

People on the outside of the caring world look nervously in and say, 'Aren't you wonderful! I do admire you. I could never do anything like that.' The facts, however, are quite different. Not only are all carers drawn from the ranks of very ordinary men and women but they do not become Mother Teresas or Florence Nightingales overnight. They begin in small ways, and then, as they gain wisdom and confidence, they find themselves drawn into deeper and deeper engagement. Like the martyrs, God chooses the weak and makes them strong in bearing witness.

Archbishop Romero, my first Good Friday person, was just such a reluctant hero. He did not set out to be a martyr but tried to keep his distance from both the military and the revolutionaries, in the way that Carol Bialock describes in her poem:

I built my house by the sea.
Not on the sands, mind you,
not on the shifting sand.
And I built it of rock.
A strong house
by a strong sea.
And we got well acquainted, the sea and I.
Good neighbours,
Not that we spoke much.
We met in silences,

respectful, keeping our distance
but looking our thoughts across the fence of sand.
Always the fence of sand our barrier,
Always the sand between.
And then one day
(and I still don't know how it happened)
The sea came.
Without warning.
Without welcome even.
Not sudden and swift, but a shifting across the sand like wine,
less like the flow of water than the flow of blood.
Slow, but flowing like an open wound.
And I thought of flight, and I thought of drowning, and I thought of death.
But while I thought the sea crept higher till it reached my door.
And I knew that there was neither flight nor death nor drowning.
That when the sea comes calling you stop being good neighbours,
Well acquainted, friendly from a distance neighbours.
And you give your house for a coral castle
And you learn to breathe under water.

Carol Bialock, Chile 1975

I have quoted this poem before in a previous book and told the story of how it was given to me by the sister who wrote it. I was so fascinated by it that I took it to work at the hospital and kept it in the pocket of my white coat, taking it out to re-read and think about when things were quiet. My first understanding of the encroachment of the sea was of the way God can take over one's life in prayer, escaping from the confines of church and Sunday and invading every aspect of life. Another interpretation is that the sea is the agony of the world and we try to keep it at a distance until it breaks through our defences and overtakes us. It is then that we have to learn to breathe under water – to be immersed in the world – or to die. Archbishop Romero was clearly speaking of this experience when he said in his famous Louvain speech: 'I am a shepherd who, with his people, has begun to learn a beautiful and difficult truth: our Christian faith requires that we *submerge* ourselves in his world.'

This, above all, is the message of Archbishop Romero, his legacy to us: that when the sea comes calling, when the pain of our world comes shifting across our fence of sand, there is no time for flight or drowning or death but we must give our home for a coral castle and learn to live under water.

And of course, the great joke and paradox is that the underwater world is very beautiful. As Jim Cotter, an Anglican priest and poet, who has experience in working with people with AIDS, writes:

> In the bearing of another's burdens,
> in the sharing of another's pain,
> we begin to dance.

The underwater dance is very beautiful because, once our eyes have become accustomed to the different light, we see things that we had never seen before. We begin to see with God's eyes, and to realize that his people are extraordinarily beautiful. I sat in church one morning quite oblivious of the sermon, recalling the events of the previous week. I thought in particular of Catherine, a forty-one year old woman with breast cancer. Catherine's man has gone off somewhere and she lives alone with her nine-year-old daughter, Cindy. It fell to me to tell Catherine that the tumour has spread to her brain and though she has very few symptoms from it at the moment, she will soon be in deep trouble. I explained that a course of radiotherapy is her only chance of buying a little more time, but even that will not cure her. She sat there, tensely, in my office, the tears beginning to fall saying quietly, 'I want whatever is best for my daughter. I don't care what I go through, if it's right for her.'

There is a rare beauty in selflessness of this kind. This is the kind of holiness I understand. This is God's love shining through a weak human being and has nothing to do with sexual abstinence or physical asceticism. This is the strange light of the underwater world: the light of the holiness of ordinary men and women who have somehow become translucent to the brightness of God.

Alas, it is not given to every sick person to reflect God's light in this way. Some people are very poor and go to their deaths grasping everything to themselves. These are the people who will call you away from another patient's deathbed to straighten their pillows or adjust the television. As I said, they are poor indeed.

It is difficult not to sit in judgement on the selfish, uncaring people of this world, let alone those who are downright wicked. It is difficult to look at those who wound us by their malice or insensitivity and see Jesus in them. And yet, he is there, as Caryll Houselander saw so clearly in this 'vision'.

> I was in an underground train, a crowded train in which all sorts of people jostled together, sitting and strap hanging – workers of every description going home at the end of the day. Quite suddenly I saw with my mind, but as vividly as a wonderful picture, Christ in them all. But I saw more than that; not only was Christ in every one of them, being in them, dying in them, rejoicing in them, sorrowing in them – but because He was in them, and because they were here, the whole world was here too in this underground train, not only the world as it was at that moment, not only all the people in all the countries of the world, but all those people who have lived in the past and all those yet to come.
>
> I came out into the street and walked for a long time in the crowds. It was the same here on every side, in every passer-by, everywhere – Christ.

This wonderfully vivid picture of Christ's life here and now in his people is the nearest I can ever get to understanding the concept of the 'Mystical Body'. Even more important, however, is this continuation of her vision:

> I saw too the reverence that everyone must have for a sinner; instead of condoning his sin, which is in reality his utmost sorrow, one must comfort Christ who is suffering in him. And this reverence must be paid even to those sinners whose souls seem to be dead, because it is Christ, who is the life of the soul, who is dead in them: they are His tombs, and Christ in the tomb is potentially the risen Christ . . .
>
> Caryll Houselander
> *A Rocking Horse Catholic*

After a few days, the vision faded and Christ was once more hidden but the impact remained: if the 'vision' had faded, the knowledge had not.

She now *knew* deep in her heart what the Gospels are always telling us: that Christ loves the sinner and he will leave the ninety-nine virtuous to do their knitting while he goes out into the hills to search for the one who has run away.

Lord, our God,
Give us the eyes to see your face
the ears to know your voice
among ordinary people,
both the good and the bad.
Let us not be fooled
by the wrapping:
by dull brown paper
or tawdry ribbon,
but grant us the insight,
the patience and gentleness,
to unwrap, to uncover,
the gifts that lie hidden
in all your people.
Help us to share the pain of others,
to learn what it means
to be fully human.

14

Pockets Shaken

We did not want it easy God,
But we did not contemplate
That it would be quite this hard,
This long, this lonely.

Anna McKenzie

Some people are called – don't ask me why – to undergo the most unspeakable suffering. They are overtaken by natural disaster, ravaged by disease, or, quite simply brutalized by their fellows. We catch glimpses of them on television or in our newspapers, their eyes wide with terror as they face death and we meet them head on in hospital wards or reports of commissions investigating war crimes. These are the suffering servants of Yahweh, men and women stripped to the bone, without beauty, without majesty, too terrible to look upon, figures to make us screen our faces lest we howl or throw up in public.

Jesus of Nazareth was one such person, for not only did his captors torture him but, before he died, they nailed him to a cross. This ultimate act of gratuitous violence symbolizes, for me, all the terrible last straws which befall or are inflicted upon suffering people before they die. It is the prising out of the last gold filling before a man goes to the gas chamber, or what Anna McKenzie sees as God turning his victims upside-down to extract their last hidden coins:

We did not want it easy God,
But we did not contemplate
That it would be quite this hard,
This long, this lonely,
So if we are to be turned inside out,

And upside down,
With even our pockets shaken,
Just to check what's rattling
And left behind . . .

What are we, the bystanders, to do with this suffering? What are we to *make* of it, what sense can we wrest from it? Like the players in an interminable game of snakes and ladders we are sent back to Go, to the square with the big question mark, and the ultimate three-letter word WHY?

Yesterday, John's wife thought he was dying, and she paced the hospice corridor like a wild animal, her face blotched and swollen with tears, clutching on to whoever would listen and demanding WHY, Why? Exhausted, we sat with her and then passed her on like a burning torch to some other comforter lest we shake her and scream, 'How the hell should I know? I'm not God.'

I have long since given up asking the 'why' of suffering. It gets me nowhere, and I know when I'm beat. I live quite peaceably in the eye of this theological storm, moving about in the accustomed darkness like a mole in its burrow or a blind woman in the safety of her home. I know less and less, but that which I *do* know, I know ever more deeply, down in my guts, where true faith lives.

What, then, is the message from this dark, still point, from the eye of the hurricane? I believe it is this: suffering *is*, in the same way that life *is*. It is a fact; denying or ignoring it will not make it go away. I do not know if it has a meaning. Deep in my heart I believe it has but I don't really know. But this I *do* know: more important than asking why, we should get in there, be alongside those who suffer. We must plunge in up to our necks in the icy water, the mud and the slurry to hold up the drowning child until he is rescued or dies in our arms. If he dies, so be it, and if we die with him, so be it also. Greater love hath no man, than he who lays down his life for his friend.

Sometimes, of course, we cannot plunge in, the sea is too wild or the flames too fierce. We are not called to sacrifice ourselves, to climb on to another's funeral pyre, but I do believe we are asked to keep vigil, to pray and to endure, to keep awake. This is what this book is about, sharing as far as we are able in the suffering of the world, which is also the suffering of God. We stand like the prisoners at Auschwitz, impotent bystanders at the execution of our fellows.

Elie Wiesel, in his chilling Nobel prize-winning book *Night*, describes the execution of two men and a young boy suspected of involvement in the sabotage of a power station.

> One day when we came back from work, we saw three gallows rearing up in the assembly place, three black crows. Roll call. SS all round us, machine guns trained: the traditional ceremony. Three victims in chains – and one of them, the little servant, the sad-eyed angel.
>
> The SS seemed more preoccupied, more disturbed than usual. To hang a young boy in front of thousands of spectators was no light matter. The head of the camp read the verdict. All eyes were on the child. He was lividly pale, almost calm, biting his lips. The gallows threw its shadow over him.
>
> This time the Lagerkapo refused to act as executioner. Three SS replaced him.
>
> The three victims mounted together on to the chairs.
>
> The three necks were placed at the same moment within the nooses.
>
> 'Long live liberty!' cried the two adults.
>
> But the child was silent.
>
> 'Where is God? Where is He?' someone behind me asked.
>
> At a sign from the head of the camp, the three chairs tipped over.
>
> Total silence throughout the camp. On the horizon, the sun was setting.
>
> 'Bare your heads!' yelled the head of the camp. His voice was raucous. We were weeping.
>
> 'Cover your head!'
>
> Then the march past began. The two adults were no longer alive. Their tongues hung swollen, blue-tinged. But the third rope was still moving; being so light, the child was still alive . . .
>
> For more than half an hour he stayed there, struggling between life and death, dying in slow agony under our eyes. And we had to look him full in the face. He was still alive

when I passed in front of him. His tongue was still red, his eyes were not yet glazed.

Behind me, I heard the same man asking:

'Where is God now?'

And I heard a voice within me answer him:

'Where is He? Here He is – He is hanging here on this gallows . . . '

Is *that* what gives meaning to suffering? Is it because God is in it, in it with us, that the obscene becomes transformed into the holy? I don't know, but I believe it is. I believe that the white transit van in which Ita Ford, Jean Donovan, Dorothy Kazel and Maura Clarke were raped and abused before they were killed was somehow hallowed because God was there, in it, more, a thousand times more than he is in any cathedral tabernacle. God is hanged in Auschwitz, he is raped and shot in El Salvador, he dies of AIDS in a London flat, and we, we pass him by like the Levite, hurrying past on our way to church.

Again and again we are caught up in the paradox, the mystery of the indwelling of God in our lives. He is the stranger dying in the gutter, the deranged Rumanian toddler bashing its head against the bars of its cot: but he is also the Samaritan lifting up our broken bodies and the gentle paediatrician clasping us weeping and soiled in his arms. What more need we know? He is there, in it, with us, in us, over and under, inside and out, a cloud of unknowing, a shield to defend us.

About fifteen years ago, in the year I came back from Chile, I had a very minor religious experience. I was spending Easter at St Beunos, a Jesuit retreat house in the Welsh Hills, where the ghost of Gerard Manley Hopkins is thought by some to lurk in the broom cupboard. I was attending the service of benediction, in which the consecrated host is exposed in the monstrance, a curious golden contraption like a sunburst. The bells rang and the incense ascended in the evening light and I gazed, as Catholics do, in bemused wonder at the tiny wafer, in its golden case. This time, however, something odd happened, because I found I could not sustain my gaze. I *felt* blinded, and was somehow forced to bow my head, because whatever it was I was looking at was too bright, too awesome, to gaze upon. That was it. That's all. No voices, no visions, just a sense of awe and wonder, a dazzling darkness on a spring afternoon.

Sometimes I wonder if the cross is like that. Extreme suffering, like the execution of the child at Auschwitz, is too awesome, too terrible, too holy for us to contemplate. We want to look elsewhere, to run away somewhere safe instead of prostrating ourselves at the feet of God.

Is this what the mediaeval artists were trying to capture, with their crosses bearing the risen, triumphant Christ? Is this what we must understand by *The Dream of the Rood*:[1]

> Listen, for I mean to tell
> of a most marvellous dream,
> which I once dreamed
> in the deep night,
> when every living soul
> was sound asleep.
> It seemed to me that I beheld
> bright in the air
> a wondrous cross of wood
> speeding its way,
> brightest of beams:
> and all that blessed sign
> glorious with gold,
> glittered with jewels,
> one on each earth – o'erstretching arm,
> and yet a fifth glowing upon its heart.
> The angel host all gazed
> lovely as God decreed,
> This was no loathesome gallows
> which all the angels saw,
> the holy souls,
> the men of earth
> and all things made by God
> To me the glorious tree appeared
> decked in solemn vestments,
> sumptuously shining,
> radiant with rich gold
> and royal jewels

adorning with glory
the Almighty's tree.
And still through all this splendour
I could see
its agonies of long ago,
as it began
to bleed from its right side.
At this strange, lovely sight
I was downcast with sorrows
and with dread.
It seemed to change,
this speeding sign,
both robes and hue;
sometimes all red with blood
running torrents,
sometimes with treasure hung.

I caught a glimpse of this paradoxical nature of the cross one evening at Ampleforth Abbey where I spent a glorious eighteen months pretending to be a monk. I sat alone in the abbey church, gazing up at the massive dark cross suspended across the transept, and found that my gaze was drawn beyond the cross to the light behind it. It was as though my immediate focus was on the dark cross but that my true gaze was drawn beyond it to the light.

I think that's how it is, or should be, with suffering. If we have the courage and the stillness of heart to keep vigil, to look into the face of a dying child, into the heart of pain, our gaze will be drawn beyond the blood, the tears and the vomit to the light of the risen Christ. This vision, of course, is a theological one, a bystander's or a hindsight understanding. You only see it when you stand back. When you're in it you are blinded by the proximity of the gallows, of the black wood, choked by the filthy gag in your mouth. That's how suffering is. It is of its essence that the sufferer is in the dark, that there seems no way out, no light at the end of the tunnel. It is then that we can only pray like Anna:

We pray that you will keep faith with us
And we with you,
Holding our hands as we weep,
Giving us strength to continue,

And showing us beacons along the way
To becoming new.

Anna McKenzie

Did God hold Ita's hand in that transit van? Surely. But did she *feel* it? I do not know. Perhaps it was necessary that she should share in the terror of the people she served, to make up what was wanting in the sufferings of Archbishop Romero who died swiftly if messily before the altar of God.

Once again we return to the Archbishop, the gentle shepherd who learned that the Church is called to submerge itself in the world and that the shepherd must share the same fate as the poor:

> Christ invites us not to fear persecution because, believe me, brothers and sisters, those who are committed to the poor must risk the same fate as the poor, and in El Salvador we know what the fate of the poor signifies: to disappear, to be tortured, to be captive and to be found dead.
>
> Archbishop Romero

Lord our God, forgive us:
we do not understand your ways.
How is it Lord, you can permit
the scandalous, terrible, devastating things
that happen to your people?
Where were you, Lord,
when the volcano erupted
on a village of people having their dinner?
Had you gone out walking, unplugged the phone?
Where are you, Lord, when the mugger strikes,
splitting an old woman's head
wide open like a breakfast egg?
Did you not hear her call your name,
beg for mercy?
Where were you, Lord?
Where were you?

15

Last Words

Father forgive them,
they know not what they do.
Luke 23:34

When he was securely nailed to the cross, the soldiers laboriously raised Jesus upright for all the world to see. It must have been a bitter sight: we glimpse him in the strange prophetic words of Isaiah's 'Fourth Song of the Servant':

> See, my servant will prosper,
> he shall be lifted up, exalted, rise to great heights.
> As the crowds were appalled on seeing him
> – so disfigured did he look
> that he seemed no longer human . . . [1]

We see him too in the Good Friday people, those men and women of sorrows, familiar with suffering:

> . . . the third rope was still moving; being so light, the child was still alive . . .
>
> For more than half an hour he stayed there, struggling between life and death, dying in slow agony under our eyes. And we had to look him full in the face . . .
>
> Elie Wiesel *Night*

Auschwitz, that monstrous blasphemy, now lies empty, a tomb both hallowed and desecrated, a terrifying monument to the madness that can erupt in a civilized society. With the Jews, we remember with shame and terror the men, women and little children who died on the gallows, in the ovens, or quietly and despairingly of lack of food.

We remember our six million dead, who died when madness ruled the world and evil dwelt on earth. We remember those we knew and those whose very name is lost. We mourn for all that died with them; their goodness and their wisdom, which could have saved the world and healed so many wounds. We mourn for the genius and the wit that died, the learning and the laughter that were lost. The world has become a poorer place and our hearts become cold as we think of the splendour that might have been. We stand in gratitude for their example of decency and goodness. They are like candles which shine out from the darkness of those years, and in their light we know what goodness is – and evil . . .

Memorial Service for the Six Million,
Jewish Prayer Book

Auschwitz lies empty, but the Son of Man is crucified always, the terrible dance continues:

> I have two more glimpses of Victor in the Stadium, two more testimonies . . . a message for me brought out by someone who was near him for some hours, down in the dressing rooms, now converted into torture chambers, a message of love for his daughters and for me . . . then once more being publicly abused and beaten, the officer nicknamed the Prince shouting at him on the verge of hysteria, losing control of himself, 'Sing now, if you can, you bastard.'[2]

And sing he did, after four days of torture and deprivation, Victor Jara raised his voice to sing for the last time, a verse from *Venceremos* – We shall overcome – the hymn of Allende's popular unity government.

Venceremos, venceremos!
Mil cadenas habra que romper,
Venceremos, venceremos!
La miseria sabemos vencer.

We shall overcome!
There are a thousand chains to break
But we shall overcome.
We know how to conquer our wretchedness.

What it cost Victor to sing this last song we shall never know – for after that they dragged him away to kill him.

There is a terrible poignancy about the last words of those about to die, an urgency and a nakedness which impel us to listen at whatever cost. The great miracle for me is the amazing selflessness with which so many people face death: their last thoughts are nearly always for the people they love, and in support of the values for which they have lived and for which they die. Thus Victor's last messages were for his wife Joan and their little girls, and then for the people of Chile: a message of hope incorporated in his final rendering of *Venceremos* and in his last poem, smuggled out of the Stadium after his death.

> What a horror the face of fascism creates!
> They carry out their plans with knife-like precision.
> Nothing matters to them.
> To them, blood equals medals,
> slaughter is an act of heroism.
> Oh God is this the world that you created,
> for this your seven days of wonder and work?
>
> We are ten thousand hands
> which can produce nothing.
> How many of us in the whole country?
> The blood of our President, our compañero
> will strike again with more strength than bombs and machine guns!
> So will our fist strike again!

Victor Jara
his last song
written in the Stadium, Chile,
September 1973

What did Victor mean by those words, I wonder: 'the blood of our President will strike again with more strength than bombs and machine guns'? Could he see, in the midst of the terror and suffering around him, that the love of the people of Chile must surely triumph over the hatred of the moment? I'm sure he did. Like Archbishop Romero he knew that the love for which he had given his life was a flame which could not be snuffed out. Like the Archbishop he could have said 'as a Christian, I don't believe in death without resurrection. If they kill me, I will rise again in the Salvadoran people. I am not boasting, or saying this out of pride, but rather as humbly as I can.'[3]

This certainty that the spirit will live on, while it sustains the dying person, does not protect him from fear and desolation. It did not protect Jesus and it will not protect us. As he hung there, Jesus struggled to articulate his final legacy to those he loved. When he had asked John to look after his mother and promised the repentant thief that this very day they would be together in paradise, he seems to have been overcome by anguish, calling out in a loud voice: 'Eli, Eli, lama sabachthani?', that is 'My God, my God, why have you forsaken me.'[4]

The scholars reassure us that this prayer is a cry of distress but not of despair because it is the opening verse of Psalm 22 in which the psalmist, after giving vent to his desolation, proclaims once more his faith in the Lord:

You are the theme of my praise in the Great Assembly,
I perform my vows in the presence of those who fear him.
The poor will receive as much as they want to eat.
Those who seek Yahweh will praise him.
Long life to their heart.[5]

Was this what Jesus would have sung, had he had the strength to continue? How can we know, for he died with the first lines on his lips?

My God, my God, why have you deserted me?
How far from saving me, the words I groan.
I call all day, my God, but you never answer,
all night long I call and cannot rest.[6]

I find this anguished cry of Jesus comforting, for this is the world I am familiar with, a world in which the protecting power of God is often completely obscured by the smoke from the crematoria of Auschwitz. We would not expect God's Son to have it any easier than his people, for as Dorothy Sayers puts it:

For whatever reason God chose to make man as he is, limited and suffering and subject to sorrows and death –

> he had the honesty and courage to take his own medicine. Whatever game he is playing with his creation, he has kept his own rules and played fair. He can extract nothing from man that he has not extracted from himself.
>
> Dorothy Sayers *Creed or Chaos*

Much more important, however, than Jesus' last words of comfort to his mother or his personal desolation is the way he prayed for his captors: 'Father, forgive them, for they know not what they do.'

I find this prayer quite stunning. Here is Jesus, stripped and brutalized, weary and afraid, about to be executed and his prayer is for his persecutors. He begs, not to be rescued, not for strength to face death with courage, but that his captors be forgiven. Like a social worker pleading for a child abuser or a delinquent teenager, he petitions the judge: 'you see, my Lord, he's not responsible, he didn't know what he was doing.'

We need to dwell long and thoughtfully upon Jesus' way of forgiveness, because it doesn't come naturally to us. Our instincts are much more in tune with the old Law, 'an eye for an eye, and a tooth for a tooth'. We want to shoot the bastards, flog the thief, castrate the rapist, hang the murderer, torture the terrorist and do all these things and more to those monsters who abuse and murder little children.

But the gospel message is embarrassingly clear. Jesus' last message was not the pious ramblings of a saint delirious with pain and exhaustion but a simple statement of how he believed sinners should be treated. We see his teaching most clearly in the Sermon on the Mount:

> But I say this to you who are listening: Love your enemies, do good to those who hate you, bless those who curse you, pray for those who treat you badly. To the man who slaps you on one cheek, present the other cheek too; to the man who takes your cloak from you, do not refuse your tunic. Give to everyone who asks you, and do not ask for your property back from the man who robs you. Treat others as you would like them to treat you. If you love those who love you, what thanks can you expect? Even sinners love those who love them . . . Instead, love your enemies and do good, and lend without any hope of return. You will

> have a great reward, and you will be sons of the Most High, for he himself is kind to the ungrateful and the wicked.

There it is. Quite unambiguous. Love your enemies. Do good to those who hate you. Doesn't make sense, does it? It's not 'natural'. But there's worse to come:

> Be compassionate as your Father is compassionate. Do not judge, and you will not be judged yourselves; do not condemn, and you will not be condemned yourselves; grant pardon and you will be pardoned. Give, and there will be gifts for you: a full measure, pressed down, shaken together, and running over will be poured into your lap; because the amount you measure out is the amount you will be given back.

I find all this very difficult to handle. Are we *really* meant to take it seriously? I think we are. And yet, if we *do* take it seriously, how should we cash it out, concretely, in our lives? Let's look at an example: a large country, led by a very powerful and charismatic leader, invades a small country and annexes it, because the acquisition of this territory gives him unimpaired access to the sea.

So what is the little country to do? Does it lie down whimpering like a dog and say: would you like my tunic as well? Surely not. Perhaps then Jesus wasn't talking about countries but about individuals. Let's try a different example. I leave my car in the station car park and go to London. When I come back, it's been broken into and various things have been stolen, including a particularly favourite navy blue sweater.

As it happens, I've never seen it again but if I did, I'm pretty sure I'd ask for it back. Or would I? I have an indecent number of navy blue sweaters: perhaps the person who nicked that one needed it. But, say he'd taken the car as well, to store his sweater in: now that's a very different issue. I have only one car and I need it and I can't afford to buy another one. So does what you do about the theft depend upon what's taken and who takes it? I don't know; nor do any of the people I've asked so far. One theologian said that these instructions were the standards of 'the Kingdom' – that fascinating, elusive concept, place, way of life that Jesus is always talking about. Most of us, said my friend, live with one foot in the Kingdom and one in the world. Some people, though, live with *both* feet in the Kingdom, and perhaps they end up as martyrs.

Take Archbishop Romero and the Maryknoll sisters in El Salvador. They had *both* feet in the Kingdom. They lived immersed in a world of violence, and yet their only response to it was to go on loving, practising the way of non-violence. We know where it landed them. But we know too the power of their lives, the power of those small flames of love which, like joke birthday candles, are quite impossible to extinguish:

> But though hate rises in enfolding flame
> At each renewed oppression, soon it dies;
> It sinks as quickly as we saw it rise,
> While love's small constant light burns still the same.
> Know this: though love is weak and hate is strong,
> Yet hate is short, and love is very long.

My commonplace book is full of such quotes, gathered from all over the world. My favourite is this Jewish saying, heard on the radio: 'We must meet extravagant and unreasonable hatred with an extravagant and unreasonable love.' What he is saying is, we must love like God: unconditionally, unilaterally, and for ever. John of the Cross knew all about God's love: 'Where there is no love', he said, 'sow love – and you will reap love.' Fine, but I like better the very pragmatic modification of the starry-eyed Carmelite's aphorism by a pragmatic Dominican working in the Peace Camps in Israel. 'Where there is no love,' he says, 'sow love, and *somebody* will reap love.'

That makes more sense to me. We must have the blind faith to be compassionate and to forgive, but we must know quite clearly that we ourselves may not live to see the tree we have planted bear fruit.

But compassion and non-violence *do* bear fruit: of that I am certain. Perhaps it would be more accurate to say that compassion and non-violent resistance to aggression *are* fruit: fruits of the spirit, free gifts of God. I believe too that forgiveness is not so much a virtue we are called to practise but a gift for which we must pray. It is too much, in the natural order of things, to demand that a mother forgive the man who raped and killed her daughter. And yet, such forgiveness is given. A man whose daughter died in his arms after a terrorist bomb attack astonished the world by declaring that he forgave her killers. I too have experienced that gift, for I knew right from the beginning that I forgave my torturers. I was able to say, quite without strain, 'Father, forgive them.' And yet it has not always been thus. Quite recently, when I was hurt by someone, I found myself possessed by bitterness and longing for revenge. Knowing myself sick, I went off in search of help, as a dog will slink off to eat grass. After I had poured out the whole messy business, the priest whom I had consulted said very quietly, 'I think the only thing you can do is pray for the power to forgive.'

So pray I did, with many bitter tears, and eventually I was able to see the situation clearly enough to let go of my wrath and re-establish dialogue with my erstwhile enemy. I can't say I went as far as turning the other cheek, but at least I sheathed my sword instead of burying it in some anatomically suitable place!

It was good for me to experience hatred, for it taught me that my power to forgive is no virtue of mine, but pure gift. I know now that I cannot demand that my brother forgive his persecutor. I cannot knock their heads together like quarrelling children and insist that they kiss and make up. I can only shower my love upon them, bury it like a seed in the dry earth and wait for the rains to come, in the sure and certain hope that he who is forgiven much will, by that very forgiveness, be freed to love.

And when from time to time, I wonder if like the social workers, I have gone too far in forgiving, I remember these words of a Victorian clergyman.

There's a wideness in God's mercy
Like the wideness of the sea.
There's a kindness in his justice
Which is more than liberty.

There's a welcome for the sinner,
And more graces for the good;
There is mercy with the Saviour;
There is healing in his blood.

For the love of God is broader
Than the measures of man's mind;
And the heart of the Eternal
Is most wonderfully kind.

But we make his love too narrow
By false limits of our own.
And we magnify its strictness
With a zeal he will not own.

If our love were but more simple,
We should take him at his word;
And our lives would all be sunshine
In the sweetness of our Lord.

F. W. Faber, 1802

I'm not quite sure about the perpetual sunshine but I am quite sure we make his love too narrow by our own mean limits.

Lord, teach us to forgive:
to look deep into the hearts
of those who wound us,
so that we may glimpse,
in that dark, still water,
not just the reflection
of our own face
but yours as well.

16

Good Friday

Still falls the rain –
Dark as the world of man, black as our loss –
Blind as the nineteen hundred and forty nails
Upon the cross.

Edith Sitwell *Still Falls the Rain*

At three o'clock on a Friday afternoon, Jesus of Nazareth died, nailed to a cross, on a hill outside Jerusalem. In historical terms, his death was a one-off event, the killing of a good man because he had somehow constituted a threat to the security of the state. Looked at in this way, Jesus' death is one of thousands of such killings and is paralleled by the deaths of many of my Good Friday people, men and women such as Rutilio Grande, Archbishop Romero, Ita Ford and Jean Donovan. It is important, I believe, if we are to wrest any meaning from Jesus' sordid and terrible death, to look at his passing in two ways: as the death of Jesus the man, one of many who have died and as Jesus the Christ, the Son of God. If we fail to do this we risk falling into one or other of two traps: despair at the awfulness of it all or worse, the 'sanitization' or glorification of suffering.

Let us look for a moment at the facts about death as far as they are available to us, and then, metaphorically holding our breath, make a colossal faith leap right into the heart of the mystery in which, like it or not, we are all involved. First, the known:

As a hospice doctor, I am all too familiar with death and *other people's* deaths hold no terror for me, for I know why and how people die and I have been present at many deaths. Men, women and children die when one of the vital bits of their 'clockwork' is irrevocably damaged. The heart may stop because its muscle is damaged and the brain will die within a few minutes because it is deprived of oxygen. It may of course happen the other way round: the brain is wounded by trauma or disease and the vital messages to heart and lungs cease to be sent. All this knowledge is fascinating to doctors and helps them 'handle' death, because, in some sense, it shields them from the overwhelming emotional and philosophical implications of the cessation of a person's life.

Each person meets death in their own way. For Archbishop Romero, death came suddenly when on 24 March 1980 he was shot at the altar, as he finished the homily at a mass for the anniversary of a friend's mother. He read the gospel from St John which speaks of how the grain of wheat must die: 'The hour has come for the Son of Man to be glorified . . . Unless the grain of wheat falls to the earth and dies, it remains only a grain. But if it dies, it bears much fruit . . . '[1] He spoke for ten minutes of the dead woman and her life, then, returning to the theme of the grain of wheat, said:

> This holy mass, this Eucharist, is an act of faith. With Christian faith we know that at this moment the wheaten host is changed into the body of the Lord, who offered himself for the world's redemption, and in this chalice the wine is transformed into the blood that was the prize of salvation. May this body immolated and this blood sacrificed for humans nourish us also, so that we may give our body and blood to suffering and to pain – like Christ, not for self, but to teach justice and peace to our people. So let us join together intimately in faith and hope at this moment of prayer for Dona Sarita and ourselves.

And then the shot rang out.

I have heard a gun fired, as I sat in prayer with a friend in Santiago – or have I? Perhaps it was the scream I remember. Or perhaps they came so close together that they were welded into one. I remember only that it was a terrible noise and my heart stood still, and I felt sick with fear. I remember too the sight of the crumpled figure on the floor and then a pool of blood getting wider and wider as I knelt there: impotently, watching her clothes turn crimson and her breathing change.

The Archbishop was shot in the heart, and he fell to the floor behind the altar, at the foot of the large crucifix. He lost consciousness immediately.

> Blood was turning the violet vestment and white alb red as the people carried him from the chapel to a small truck outside. Down the drive, down the street, down the hill it went, five minutes to the Policlinica hospital.
>
> In the emergency room, he lay on a table . . . still unconscious, as the nurse on emergency room duty probed for a vein in his arm to start a transfusion . . . In a few minutes he stopped gasping and he was dead.[2]

It was the vigil of the Feast of the Annunciation, the celebration of Mary's 'fiat', her yes, to God's call. It's a day which people choose to enter convents, to be ordained or to make their vows, so perhaps it's a fitting day to die. Again and again we find ourselves caught up in this dual reality of death: the mess, the tragedy, the violence, the sheer wickedness of it all, and then, the mysterious flip side, the deeper mystical reality, the amazing beauty of a death in which a human being gives his or her life for another.

T. S. Eliot captures it in Thomas a Becket's Christmas Day sermon in *Murder in the Cathedral*, in which he draws our attention to the curious fact that the feast of the first martyr, St Stephen, comes hot on the heels of Christmas Day. It is no accident, he tells his congregation, that the Church celebrates these two apparently different feasts so closely together, for just as we both rejoice and mourn in the birth and passion of our Lord, so in like manner, we both rejoice and mourn at the death of a martyr. We mourn both the loss of the person who has died and the violence of those who killed them but at the same time we rejoice that another soul is numbered among the saints.

I remember when, in the December of 1980, I learned of Ita Ford's death in Salvador, thinking not *just* 'how awful', but also, 'how amazing, Ita's a martyr, like Romero, like Polycarp, like Thomas a Becket.'

Always, always, there is this double knowledge: the carnal and the mystical. I have watched too often on film the uncovering of Ita's grave, and the terrible dragging out of the bodies of those four women. Their friends stand grimly by, hands over mouths, as the ropes tauten and each body is brought out. One shares just a little, each time, in the agony of these people and in the experience of all who must identify the three-day remains of those they love. One is overcome by the senselessness of these deaths: four women who were killed because they cared for refugees and orphans, and whose unconditional love was interpreted as sedition.

It's the unconditional love, of course, which is the key to the mystical understanding of these deaths, for it is in these martyrs that we catch a glimpse of what it means to be a saint.

As Eliot's Becket tells his people, we do not think of the martyr as someone killed simply because he was a good Christian – for that would only be a cause for mourning. Neither, however, do we think of him or her simply as a good Christian who has gone to heaven – for that would be a cause for rejoicing. No. Our mourning and our rejoicing are inseparable, for a martyrdom is always by God's design, born of his love for his people. A martyrdom is 'never the design of man; for the true martyr is he who has become the instrument of God, who has lost his will in the will of God, and who no longer desires anything for himself, not even the glory of being a martyr.' So it is that the Church both mourns and rejoices at the same time, in a way that the world cannot understand.

I have tried, in earlier chapters, to show the way in which a number of my Good Friday people have 'lost' their will in God's will, have submerged themselves in him, not by walling themselves up in the desert but by 'learning to live under water', by submerging themselves in the pain of the world.

Father Daniel Berrigan, a Jesuit active in the United States' peace movement, describes this submerging of the will, the making of a saint, like this:

> The saints were not born as isolated phenomena, but as kneaded and pressed into a common mould and feature: into the communion of saints. And the saint, as a member of the Church, may be defined as one in whom the double operation of knowledge and love of Jesus Christ has shown most gloriously. It is the saint who knows Christ most accurately: precisely because that knowledge, a gift of

> grace, has passed over instantaneously to love: knowledge and love have been pressed by the anguish of life into a single living ferment.

I love that image: a single living *ferment*, a leaven, a yeast, to give life to a people flattened by oppression and despair.

> With grace enlightening their minds and wills, humanity finds in them a new possibility. It is true that in certain of them, knowledge of sources and development of dogma, of the Divine scheme of things may have been minimal from a scientific point of view: but their love was always divinely excessive: more, their knowledge of the science of life, its inner meaning has an accuracy, an intensity, an inner serenity that mark it as the product of grace. Because they know human life, they go without danger into any area of life: in the Church the paradoxes of grace are commonplace: the unlettered saint confounding the doctors: the doctor upon the scaffold: the man or woman of extraordinary social talent finding fulfilment in contemplative obscurity: the contemplative leading a crusade, the child confounding the tyrant, the old man singing a song in the fire of martyrdom, the mystic sitting down with princes: the prince in the hair shirt, the hermit returning to set the kingdom aright.

The right wing Archbishop become a human rights' champion: the rich American socialite caring for Salvadoran orphans: the nun raped and shot in the back of a van: the Chilean singer tortured because he sang of freedom for the poor: the dancer who used her last weeks of life to beg for understanding of people with AIDS . . .

> In all of them a Divine principle has come to flower: an inner logic is directing things to a divine outcome: in all of them the Church is mediating Jesus in time, is still bringing forth, with a truly divine fecundity, the sons and daughters who bear Christ into the world.

Dan Berrigan *The Bride*

Inseparable from the physical annihilation and the mystical elements of death there is another vital dimension: the grief of those left behind.

'Near the cross of Jesus stood his mother and his mother's sister, Mary the wife of Clopas, and Mary of Magdala.'[3] John was there, too, and we see him in mediaeval art supporting the weeping Mary in his arms.

The grief of Mary is a favourite subject for painters and poets for she forms an archetype for all who have lost a child. I love the following lines from a long poem written in 1928 by the Russian poet Aleksej Remizov. It is called *The Star of Stars* and he describes it as 'my love song for the Mother of God . . . born out of the suffering of our times . . . '

In the Annunciation of the Passion he portrays the outrage of the Archangels Gabriel, Michael and Raphael as God tries to persuade each of them in turn to tell Mary that her son must die:

> The archangels, cherubim and seraphim grew fearful: the powers of heaven trembled.
> Dumb-founded, the angels who watch over all things, shut their eyes.
> Who will go to the Mother of God?
> Who will bear this terrible news to her?
> Who will announce the irrevocable will of Almighty God who from the beginning condemned the Son?

Each in turn they are asked, and each feels unequal to the task.

> In fear and trembling, their blazing white wings crossed
> the one over the other,
> tears flowing from their burning bright eyes . . .

The angels dig in their toes. Breaking bad news is not their job. At last, it is a small bird, a linnet, who after hearing the celestial weeping, alerts Mary to the passage of her son on his way to Golgotha.

> Down came the linnet to earth.
> He flew down to the Mother of God
> and alighted on the window sill,
> nodding his head like a sunflower,
> and he began to sing.
> How sadly he sang!

The Mother of God lifts up her eyes and sees suddenly the

terrible face of Judas Iscariot: his eyes wild and despairing, as he stands beneath her window.

> The Mother of God arose
> but fell back again upon the window seat,
> the linnet sang sadly,
> woeful little bird.
> Anguish enveloped her, and pierced to the heart
> by a horrifying presentiment,
> the Mother of God ran to the door.

And there, in the crowded street, she sees her son, walking slowly along the road to Golgotha, the place of execution.

> Who will comfort a mother who has lost her son?
> Who will give her refuge?
> Who will shelter her in the dark night of grief?
> To whom can she turn?
> – the linnet, terrified by the shouting
> flies away,
> the lips of the beloved disciple
> are sealed by grief.
> Who will console her?
> She is alone, the Mother of God.

On and on it goes, in the terrible way that grief goes on and on. Loss of a child is not a problem to be solved, something one can 'get closure' on, it is an open wound, a change of status, an amputation which scars over but never really heals.

> Who will comfort a mother
> from whom a son has been snatched away?
> Who will give her refuge?
> Who will shelter her in the dark night of grief?
> They say: 'Go home.'
> Who will lead her to her home?
> Who will stay with her in her sorrow?
> Who will pay heed to the cries of her heart?

Perhaps it is the grief of parents, the anguish of widowers that is the worst part of death, for however much we believe that 'the souls of the virtuous are in the hands of God', and 'No torment shall ever touch them'[4] the grief remains and our hearts are pierced by a sword that is turned again and again by each passing memory.

> White and slender as a birch tree,
> the Mother of God was bowed to the rock
> at the foot of the cross,
> and she begged and pleaded:
> let me die!
> She could not face any person, nor the world.
> She had no wish to get up.
> – the heart of the Mother of Sorrows was desolate,
> Consumed by anguish,
> O burning coals of fire
> her heart is laid waste,
> her spirit extinguished.
> Most sorrowful am I among all mothers!
> Most sorrowful am I among all the creatures of earth!
>
> Aleksej Remizov *The Star of Stars*

Lord, we pray for those who mourn,
for parents and children,
husbands and lovers,
friends and neighbours.
Be gentle with them in their grief.
Show them the depths of your love,
a glimpse of the Kingdom of heaven.
Spare them the torment
of guilt and despair,
be with them as they weep,
beside the empty tomb.

17

Darkness over the Land

The clear light of day grew black
– the sun expired!
The stars appeared and against the blackness
they flickered like emeralds
Then came a noise like thunder and they were extinguished.
Disconsolate, the moon disappeared.
The earth shook.
The seas, the lakes and rivers boiled,
The grasses of the fields trembled.
The oak-wood rustled.
The forests bowed down.
The apple blossom shook and the catkins of the birch tree
The dry stump snapped.
Prostrate, arms outstretched in the shape of a cross
– a flaming brand in the middle of a cornfield –
the Mother of God lay at the foot of the cross.

Aleksej Remizov *The Star of Stars*

I had thought, in my innocence, to write clearly and concisely of the mystery of Jesus' death but when it comes to the moment I don't know where to begin. Perhaps that is the way of theology, the way of mysteries: it is like a stained glass window, a painting or a poem, a patchwork quilt, a Persian rug: there is a riot of colour, a brilliant pattern, but no obvious way 'in'. I have become both entranced and confused by this particular mystery, moving backwards and forwards between Scripture old and new, canonical and apocryphal, and liturgy, Roman and Byzantine, until I am both dizzy and exhausted. All I can do is to take hold of a single thread and follow it slowly to see where it leads me.

Let me begin, then, with John. His account of the death of

Jesus is amazingly brief: after he has been given a drink of vinegar, Jesus says, 'It is accomplished', bows his head and dies. That's it. And I imagine that's how it was. John was there: he saw it happen. Death is often like that: a quiet letting go, so that it takes a while to realize that what a minute ago was a living breathing human being is now, quite simply, a shell.

The synoptic Gospels, however, especially Matthew, have much more to say and from their description has grown an amazing and beautiful tradition of liturgy and art as Christians have struggled, over the years, to make sense of the deepest reality of their faith: the death and resurrection of the Son of God. Let's look now at Matthew, who sees the scene much more dramatically: 'From the sixth hour [midday] there was darkness over all the land until the ninth hour [three o'clock in the afternoon].'[1]

How are we to take this description? Was there a storm, or an eclipse, or is the Evangelist speaking symbolically? It seems most likely that Matthew is using 'darkness' as an image to convey the appalling reality of what was happening – although in the Gospel of Peter we read, 'Now it was noon day, and darkness prevailed over all Judea . . . And many went about with lamps, supposing it was night, and fell.'[2]

There is more to come: 'the veil of the Temple was torn in two from top to bottom; the earth quaked, the rocks were split, and the tombs opened and the bodies of many holy men rose from the dead, and these, after his resurrection, came out of their tombs, entered the Holy City and appeared to a number of people.'[3]

What on earth are we to make of all that? Perhaps we should avoid the temptation to say, 'Did it really happen?' and ask instead, 'What was Matthew getting at?' What was he trying to tell us? And perhaps, what did the early church make of it?

First, the veil of the temple. Here we must go right back to Exodus, where Yahweh makes a Covenant with Moses and comes to live among the people of Israel.

> Yahweh said to Moses, 'Come up to me on the mountain and stay there while I give you the stone tablets – the law and the commandments – that I have written for their

> instruction'. Accordingly Moses rose, he and his servant Joshua, and they went up the mountain of God . . . The cloud covered the mountain, and the glory of Yahweh settled on the mountain of Sinai; for six days the cloud covered it, and on the seventh day Yahweh called to Moses from inside the cloud. To the eyes of the sons of Israel the glory of Yahweh seemed like a devouring fire on the mountain top. Moses went right into the cloud. He went up the mountain and stayed there for forty days and forty nights.[4]

Forty days and forty nights Moses spent in 'retreat' with Yahweh, just as Jesus was to spend forty days in the desert in preparation for his mission. During that time, it seems, Yahweh gave Moses instructions for construction of the sanctuary, his future dwelling-place, and how he was to be worshipped. In the centre of the sanctuary was to be placed the ark, an acacia-wood box plated on the inside with pure gold, which was to hold the two stone tablets on which were written God's commandments for his people. On top of the ark they were to construct a golden throne, the throne of mercy for, 'There I shall come to meet you, there, from above the throne of mercy, from between the two cherubs that are on the ark of the Testimony, I shall give you all my commands for the sons of Israel.'[5]

This ark and its precious contents, Yahweh instructed, were to be placed in a tabernacle, a very grand and beautiful tent which was divided into two compartments, a sort of outer and an inner chamber. The ark was to be placed in the inner sanctum, the Holy of Holies, hidden from view by a splendid *veil*: 'You are to make a veil of purple stuffs, violet shade and red, of crimson stuffs, and of fine twined linen; you are to have it finely embroidered with cherubs.'[6] Eventually, it was all ready, and Yahweh came to take possession of his sanctuary. 'The cloud covered the Tent of Meeting and the glory of Yahweh filled the tabernacle. Moses could not enter the Tent of Meeting because of the cloud that rested on it and because of the glory of Yahweh that filled the tabernacle.'[7]

And so, Yahweh came to live among the people of Israel, they became his people and he became their God. Slowly but surely he led them through the desert:

> At every stage of their journey, whenever the cloud rose

> from the tabernacle the sons of Israel would resume their march. If the cloud did not rise, they waited and would not march until it did. For the cloud of Yahweh rested on the tabernacle by day, and a fire shone within the cloud by night, for all the House of Israel to see. And so it was for every stage of their journey.[8]

Eventually, four hundred and eighty years after the Israelites came out of the land of Egypt, King Solomon (following in Moses' footsteps as leader of the people of Israel) began to build a temple for Yahweh in Jerusalem. It was a very grand temple made of stone and cedar wood, and 'In the inner part of the Temple he designed a Debir [a Sanctuary – the Holy of Holies] to contain the ark of the covenant of Yahweh.'[9] And Yahweh came to live in the temple, in the Holy of Holies, behind the sacred veil, and he promised Solomon, 'if you follow my statutes and obey my ordinances and faithfully follow my commandments . . . I will make my home among the sons of Israel, and never forget Israel my people.'[10]

When King Solomon had finished his building programme: the temple, his own palace and so on, Yahweh appeared to him for the second time with a promise and a warning:

> I consecrate this house you have built: I place my name there for ever; my eyes and my heart shall always be there. . . . But if you turn away from me, you or your sons, and do not keep the commandments and laws I have set before you, and go and serve other gods and worship them, then I will cut Israel off from the land I have given them, and I will cast out from my presence this Temple that I have consecrated for my name, and Israel shall become a proverb and a byword among all the nations.[11]

Now Solomon died around 931 BC, over nine hundred years before the birth of Jesus, but the temple continued to be the holy place for the Jews, the place where Yahweh lived and where they worshipped. The ark of the Covenant continued in the Holy of Holies, hidden from all but the High Priest by the veil, the veil of the temple.

So, when Matthew says that the 'veil of the Temple was torn in two from top to bottom' it is no wonder that he adds in that the earth quaked and the tombs opened because he is making a terrible statement: that the old Mosaic cult is destroyed, and that Yahweh no longer dwells in the temple.

It is the end of the old Law. Yahweh has made a new Covenant with his people, he and his Son have made their home, not in a tent, nor yet in a temple but in the hearts of ordinary men and women.

This theme of the veil and the new Covenant is picked up and elaborated in the Letter to the Hebrews, written probably around forty years after the death of Christ. The author sees Christ as 'the high priest of all the blessings which were to come' who 'has passed through the greater, the more perfect tent'[12] into the true Sanctuary of God. Unlike the priests of the old Law, who had to offer sacrifice again and again to ask forgiveness for their own sins and those of the people, Christ, the great High Priest, has offered himself as the perfect sacrifice to God. 'He has made his appearance once and for all, now at the end of the last age, to do away with sin by sacrificing himself.'[13]

This theme of Christ as the High Priest who has sacrificed himself for our sins is a pivotal one in the liturgy of Good Friday both in the Roman and the Byzantine rites occurring both in Matins and in the Liturgy of the Word. It is in the Good Friday afternoon service that we meet the wonderfully comforting image of Christ as a man like ourselves. True, he is a priest, indeed the great High Priest, but he has been taken from among the people, flesh of our flesh, spirit of our spirit. 'It is not as if we had a high priest who was incapable of feeling our weaknesses with us; but we have one who has been tempted in every way that we are, though he is without sin.'[14] We are not to be afraid of him because of his priestly status but 'Let us be confident, then, in approaching the throne of grace, that we shall have mercy from him and find grace when we are in need of help.'[15]

I love this image of Christ the priest because it fits so closely with my own experience of those men whose priesthood has been precious to me. I have always been impatient with the image of the priest as a man set apart, holier than his people, to be revered and cosseted, protected by a dragon housekeeper or his impeccable black suit.

I remember so well going to see one of the Chilean bishops

one grey afternoon, in search of help for a young man who was on the run. We found him at home, in an L-shaped room which had his bed at one end and an altar at the other. He was a shabby man, dressed in an old sweater and a poncho, trying rather miserably to cope with a heavy cold. He listened carefully to us and made helpful suggestions, although I forget now what they were. I suspect Archbishop Romero was not unlike him.

I think that we, the people, have much to learn from the Latin American Church and from its pastors. I love this prayer of Bishop Eduardo Pironio from Argentina:

> Mother of those on Pilgrimage,
> We are the People of God, in Latin America,
> We are the Church, on a Journey towards Easter.
> We ask you:
> That our Bishops should have the heart of a father,
> That our priests be friends of God for the people,
> That our religious show forth the anticipated joy of the Kingdom of Heaven,
> that our people should be witness of the risen Lord.
> And that we should all walk together, side by side with all men,
> Sharing their anguish and their hope.
> May the people of Latin America go forward together along the paths of peace and justice.
>
> from *Nuestra Senora de America*

I find in Bishop Pironio's words a wonderful blueprint for living, a gospel blueprint for the Church and it reminds me of the prayer of another powerful clergyman, Lord George McLeod, the venerable old man who founded the Iona Community.

> We bless thee, O God, for the Church at Home.
> It's often too frail for the modern storm, is that Church at Home
> Too conformist for a world that's dying
> Too respectable for the drunkard or wretch to feel at home there
> Too concerned for its money to proclaim the prophetic and scarifying

word of peace as the only way for the world;
We ask Thee, O God, so to invade that Church at Home
that it becomes more careful of drunkards
more courageous for peace
more acquisitive of love;
And, just because each one of us is that Church at Home,
Help us to view again our attitude to money in the light of
Thy poverty
Our attitude to drunkards and the lecherous in the light of
Thy love for them
and our attitude to war in the light of Thy so strange way
of dealing with it;
Lest, when we speak so critically of the frailty of the Church
at Home
in our walks we should suddenly confront Thee, Lord
Christ,
Suddenly at the bend of the road,
and not escape Thy silent gaze at us,
Thy silent gaze at each one of us,
so clearly saying:
You are the cause of the frailty of the Church at Home.

This prayer always makes me feel like the wretched Job, after Yahweh has given him an earful from the heart of the tempest:[16]

I am the man who obscured your designs
with my empty-headed words.
I have been holding forth on matters I cannot understand,
on marvels beyond me and my knowledge.

I retract all I have said,
and in dust and ashes I repent.[17]

I take comfort, however, from my heroine, the ever-questioning Annie Dillard, who in the midst of her search for answers to the problem of suffering writes, 'Who are we to demand explanations of God? (And what monsters of perfection should we be if we did not?)'[18]

Lord of the Universe
Word of Life,

open to us
the riches of your teaching.
Lead us ever deeper
into the mystery
of who you are
and where you are leading us.
Spirit of God,
open our hearts
to the wonders of your law.

18

The Day of the Lord

Prostrate, arms outstretched in the shape of a cross
– a flaming brand in the middle of a cornfield –
the Mother of God lay at the foot of the cross.
The dead rose out of their graves:
– out of the graveyard they began to walk
to the outskirts of the city;
in the squares and at the crossroads
they mingled with the living.
A cold wind blew. Frost descended.
In the darkness, in a fearful whirlwind
wild, tempestuous gusts rushed whistling about
Noises resounded, like iron being hammered in a forge
Shrieks and groans echoed.
Burning darts split the heavens,
and the air was stirred up in vile flurries.
From end to end the temple shook;
and the veil of the temple was torn
– not a stone was left upon a stone.

Aleksej Remizov *The Star of Stars*

Matthew's account of the raising of the dead (absent from the other Gospels) is brought marvellously to life in Remizov's poem. The Siberian wind howls in the graveyard and there are noises off of iron being hammered. Where does this imagery come from, we ask, and where is it taking us?

I find myself forgetting, again and again, as I read the Gospels that not only are they telling us a story but they are trying to teach, to make sense, for themselves and their listeners of what they have seen and heard and felt. Whether Jesus' life slipped quietly away on the cross and all the bystanders went home to tea or whether there was a cosmic upheaval, as Matthew suggests, is, in a sense, immaterial. What really matters is that Matthew, and the church which grew out of this motley group of men, was utterly convinced that this was the most important day in history: the day of the coming of Yahweh.

The day of Yahweh is an enormously powerful and fascinating theme which runs throughout the Old Testament, particularly through the prophets. We meet it first in the second chapter of Isaiah:

> Get among the rocks,
> hide in the dust,
> at the sight of the terror of Yahweh,
> at the brilliance of his majesty,
> when he arises
> to make the earth quake.
>
> Human pride will lower its eyes,
> the arrogance of men will be humbled.
> Yahweh alone shall be exalted,
> on that day.
> Yes, that will be the day of Yahweh Sabaoth . . . [1]

We meet it again and again in the later prophets, the foretelling of a terrible day of reckoning when those who oppress the poor and the needy will find retribution:

> That day – it is the Lord Yahweh who speaks –
> I will make the sun go down at noon,
> and darken the earth in broad daylight.
> I am going to turn your feasts into funerals,
> all your singing into lamentation;
> I will have your loins all in sackcloth,
> your heads all shaved.
> I will make it a mourning like the mourning for an only son,
> as long as it lasts it will be like a day of bitterness.
> Amos 8:9f

Of particular interest is Zephaniah's account of the day of the Lord, for it is from this that Thomas of Celano (c. 1250) derives his famous dirge, the *Dies Irae*.

First, Zephaniah:

The great day of Yahweh is near,
near, and coming with all speed.
How bitter the sound of the day of Yahweh,
the day when the warrior shouts his cry of war,
A day of wrath, that day,
a day of distress and agony,
a day of ruin and of devastation,
a day of darkness and gloom,
a day of cloud and blackness,
a day of trumpet blast and battle cry
against fortified town
and high corner-tower.
On the day of the anger of Yahweh,
in the fire of his jealousy,
all the earth will be consumed.
For he means to destroy, yes, to make an end
of all the inhabitants of the earth.[2]

Two thousand years later, his ideas are taken up in a funeral hymn:

Dies irae, dies illa
Solvet saeclum in favilla
Teste David cum Sibylla.
Day of wrath and doom impending,
David's word with Sibyl's blending
Heaven and earth in ashes ending.
Thomas of Celano *Dies Irae*

But – the day Jesus died clearly was *not* the end of the world, so what happened? Here we must go to the first epistle of St Peter to begin to unearth the origin of a very ancient theological concept: the descent of Christ into hell.

Peter does not make a big thing of it, but slips the idea in the middle of an exhortation to his disciples, the gentile Christians of Asia Minor, telling them not to lose heart if they are persecuted for doing what is right, because Christ himself suffered in this way: 'Why, Christ himself, innocent though he was, had died once for sins, died for the guilty, to lead us to God. In the body he was put to death, in the spirit he was raised to life, and, in the spirit, he went to preach to the spirits in prison.'[3] Here we have the scriptural foundation for what was to become one of the 'articles' of the Apostles' Creed: Christ's descent into hell,

> I believe in God, the Father Almighty,
> creator of heaven and earth.
> I believe in Jesus Christ, his only Son, our Lord.
> He was conceived by the power of the Holy Spirit,
> and born of the Virgin Mary.
> He suffered under Pontius Pilate,
> was crucified, died and was buried.
> He descended to the dead.
> On the third day he rose again.
> He ascended into heaven,
> and is seated at the right hand of the Father.
> He will come again to judge the living and the dead.

In this brief allusion of Peter to Christ's descent into hell, we have the echo of Jesus' promise to the apostle when he appointed him as guardian of his Church: 'You are Peter and on this rock I will build my Church. And the gates of the underworld can never hold out against it. I will give you the keys of the kingdom of heaven.'[4]

The gates of the underworld – what does Jesus mean? Descended to the dead – what are we talking about? How, I ask myself, can I have lived more than fifty years of my life as a Christian, a practising Roman Catholic, saying the Creed every time I go to mass, and never asked that question before? Now, though, I *have* asked it and the answers that have come to me have illuminated my faith in a quite unexpected way. I feel almost as though I have become a Christian for the first time; moved from being a worshipper of the unseen, transcendent God to include in my gaze his only Son. While my worship remains theocentric I now understand much more clearly the theology behind my favourite Easter hymn:

> This joyful Eastertide,
> away with sin and sorrow,
> my love, the Crucified
> hath sprung to life this morrow.
> Had Christ that once was slain,
> ne'er burst his three day prison:

Our faith had been in vain:
but now hath Christ arisen.
George Ratcliffe Woodward (1849–1934)
This Joyful Eastertide

'Our faith had been in vain' is an echo of Paul's message to the people of Corinth who were doubting the Christian teaching of life after death. Paul becomes exasperated with them:

> Now if Christ raised from the dead is what has been preached, how can some of you be saying that there is no resurrection of the dead? If there is no resurrection of the dead, Christ himself cannot have been raised, and if Christ has not been raised then our preaching is useless, and your believing it is useless; . . . For if the dead are not raised, Christ has not been raised, and if Christ has not been raised, you are still in your sins. And what is more serious, all who have died in Christ have perished. If our hope in Christ has been for this life only, we are the most unfortunate of all people.[5]

I love Paul's realism: if Christ did not rise from the dead, then all that we are teaching is nonsense. Our whole card house of faith is built on that belief. Christ is the cornerstone: remove him and the whole house collapses.

It is because of the pivotal nature of the Apostles' teaching on the resurrection that we must look much more closely at what they believed happened that Friday afternoon when Jesus died. Clearly, they believed, something amazing and wonderful occurred – but that something was hidden and mysterious so the only way they could describe the impact of it upon themselves was to draw upon the most dramatic imagery in their tradition: the Day of the Coming of the Lord. They saw Christ as the victorious conqueror who would lay waste the wicked oppressor and rescue his people from bondage. The canticle of the prophet Habakkuk, used in the liturgy for Good Friday, is a wonderful example of this imagery of God the warrior. It begins with a *theophany*, a manifestation of God's splendour and power such as we see when God 'shows' himself to Moses on Mount Sinai, at the baptism of Jesus in the Jordan or at the transfiguration.

God comes forth from Teman,
The Holy One comes from Mount Paran.
His splendour covers the sky
and his glory fills the earth.
His brilliance is like the light,
rays flash from his hands;
there his power is hidden.

Plague goes in front of him,
fever follows on his heels,

When he stands up he makes the earth tremble,
with his glance he makes the nations quake.

Then the ancient mountains are dislodged,
the everlasting hills sink down,
his pathway from of old.[6]

The triumphant progress of Yahweh at the head of his conquering army echoes the way the Lord marched with his people in the desert in the Exodus, leading them out of captivity. There is a terrible storm, the rains come and the flood waters rage and boil:

You trench the soil with torrents;
the mountains shiver when they see you,
great floods sweep on their way,
the abyss roars aloud,
high it lifts its hands.[7]

There can be few people, surely, even modern, grown-up, scientific people who have not trembled in awe during a violent storm, and wondered what, in a cosmic sense, was going on behind it all. It is hardly surprising that our forefathers interpreted it as God flexing his muscles!

The darkness thence returns:

Sun and moon stay in their houses,
avoiding the flash of your arrows,
the gleam of your glittering spear.

Raging, you stride the earth,
in anger you trample the nations.[8]

Nearly three thousand years after Habakkuk, a passionate New York woman, Julia Ward Howe, used his imagery in a song of her own, 'The Battle Hymn of the Republic', written during the stormy days of the American Civil War:

> Mine eyes have seen the glory of the coming of the Lord
> He is trampling out the vintage where the grapes of wrath are stored;
> He hath loosed the fateful lightening of his terrible swift sword:
> His truth is marching on.

Julia Howe knew her theology, however, for she sees Christ at the head of his heavenly army, calling sinners to judgement:

> He hath sounded forth the trumpet that shall never call retreat;
> He is sifting out the hearts of man before his judgement seat:
> Oh, be swift, my soul, to answer him, be jubilant my feet!
> Our God is marching on.

So Yahweh, the conqueror, the avenger, comes, not just to trample all before him, not simply to punish the wicked but to rescue the oppressed. This is the Messiah for whom the Jews have waited impatiently for nearly two thousand years. They are convinced, against all odds, that he will come. The following, most famous verse from Habakkuk, is a statement of faith and hope against all odds: whatever happens, war, famine, persecution, they will continue to trust in the Lord:

> For even though the fig does not blossom,
> nor fruit grow on the vine,
> even though the olive crop fail,.
> and the fields produce no harvest,
> even though the flocks vanish from the folds
> and stalls stand empty of cattle,
>
> Yet I will rejoice in the Lord,
> and exult in God my Saviour.
> The Lord is my strength.
> He makes me leap like the deer
> he guides me to the high places.[9]

This last passage from the canticle of Habakkuk is much used in liturgy because it captures so well the essence of Christian hope: that, whatever happens, the Lord will give us strength and joy, and he will guide us to high places. His words somehow foreshadow the amazing words of Paul in Romans 8, words which I made my own during three weeks of solitary confinement:

> Nothing therefore can come between us and the love of Christ, even if we are troubled or worried, or being persecuted, or lacking food or clothes, or being threatened or even attacked. As Scripture promised: For your sake we are being massacred daily, and reckoned as sheep for the slaughter. These are the trials through which we triumph, by the power of him who loved us.
>
> For I am certain of this: neither death nor life, no angel, no prince, nothing that exists, nothing still to come, not any power, or height or depth, nor any created thing, can ever come between us and the love of God made visible in Jesus our Lord.[10]

Once again, we come back to the question of the psalmist, 'from where shall come my help?', on what do we base our hope, upon what did Paul base his unconquerable faith? The answer lies in that secret happening, that hidden time that lies between Good Friday and Easter Day: the time when Christ descended among the dead and, in doing that, overcame the powers of evil and death, so that we may sing:

> O death, where is thy victory?
> O death, where is thy sting?[11]

God of our Fathers, Lord of Life,
We believe in you.
We believe you lived, a man like us,
and we know you died, a messy death,
while your friends stood helpless by.
Lord, we believe, (don't ask us how)
that you rose again –
somehow transformed, glorious and immortal,
yet still yourself.

We dare to believe, because of you,
that we too shall rise,
most wonderfully changed.
Yet still ourselves, to be with you.
Lord, help our unbelief.

19

The Harrowing of Hell

Hades was embittered when it tasted of his flesh
It received a body, and it encountered God.
It received earth, and came face to face with heaven.
O death, where is thy sting? O Hades, where is thy victory?

Ancient Homily for Easter Day
attributed to St John Chrysostom

Over five thousand years ago, three thousand years before the beginnings of Christianity, a group of primitive farmers settled down on the fertile plain between two rivers, in the land that we now call Iraq. The rivers were the Tigris and the Euphrates and the land between them was called Mesopotamia: 'the land between the rivers', it was here that the earliest civilization, the land of Sumer, developed between 4000 and 3500 BC.

The Sumerian civilization developed rapidly, and within a thousand years the Sumerians had bronze implements, wheeled vehicles, sailing vessels, sculpture, monumental buildings and most important for their survival, the plough. There are written records from as early as 3000 BC and from these we learn that the Sumerians were also a people with a highly developed theological system.

Their basic idea was simple: the major natural forces, earth and sky, water, wind, fire, and so on, were personified and endowed with enormous power, including the power of eternal life. The gods were ruled by Anu, the god of the sky and each year they met on New Year's Day to decide what would happen during the coming year. Their decisions were carried out by Enlil, the God of Storms and Thunder, who punished and brought disaster according to the will of the gods.

Just as the Sumerians made sense of their life by a supernatural world of gods of the living, they made sense of death by developing the concept of an underworld, a terrible 'Land of no return', a land of the dead.

> Under the earth, beyond the abyss of the Apsu lay the infernal dwelling place to which men descended after death. It was the 'Land of no return', 'the house from which he who enters does not come out' . . . To enter it a man had successively to penetrate seven gates, abandoning at each a part of his apparel. When the last gate closed behind him he found himself naked and imprisoned forever in the 'dwelling place of the shadows'.[1]

We get a glimpse of this land of shadows when Enkidu, the companion of the ancient Sumerian hero Gilgamesh, is allowed to visit it and return. It was a sad picture. In these regions of eternal darkness the souls of the dead – edimmu – 'clad like birds in a garment of wings' are all jumbled together:

> In the house of dust
> Live lord and priest
> Live the wizard and the prophet . . .
> Live those whom the great gods
> Have anointed in the abyss.
> Dust is their nourishment
> And their food is mud.
>
> *The Myth of Creation* (1000 BC)

This ancient Sumerian image of the dwelling-place of the dead is considered to be the common source of later mythological visions of the universe of both East and West and it is from these ideas that the Old Testament concept of Sheol or Hades was developed.

We first hear mention of Sheol in Genesis when, after the apparent death of his beloved son Joseph, Jacob mourns: 'Jacob, tearing his clothes and putting on a loincloth of sackcloth, mourned his son for a long time. All his sons and daughters came to comfort him, but he refused to be comforted. "No," he said, "I will go down in mourning to Sheol, beside my son." And his father wept for him.'[2]

It seems that this concept of Sheol or the underworld as a place for the dead was common currency among a diverse group of peoples. We get the clearest picture of it from Greek mythology where Sheol is known as Hades, the mournful abode where, separated from their bodies, the souls of those who had finished their earthly existence took refuge. Initially, 'The Afterworld' was thought to be at the ends of the earth, beyond the vast ocean and encircled by a great river which had to be crossed in order to reach the desolate and uncultivated shore of the infernal regions. There, few things grew, the soil was barren and no living being could survive, for the sun's rays could not penetrate it. Black poplars were found there, and willows which never bore any fruit.

I find this description of Hades chillingly familiar for it echoes the descriptions of prison in literature the world over:

> Right there,
> where the light of the sun
> lost itself
> more than a century ago,
> where all gaiety is impossible
> and any smile
> is a grimace of irony,
> where the stone stench of darkness
> inhabits those corners
> even the spiders
> have abandoned as inhospitable,
> and where human pain eludes
> that which can be called human
> and enters the category
> of the unprintable –
> There I am writing.
>
> Public Jail, Santiago, Chile
> July 1974

Unlike *Tartarus*, the torture chamber, the underworld was thought of as a place of perpetual internment rather than punishment. It was presided over by Hades, a cold deity who ruthlessly applied the rules of his kingdom to all without discrimination. The dead were regarded as mere shadows of their living selves, who lacked blood and consciousness, and dwelt in the underworld without escape for ever, generally pursuing the activities of their former life in a wan, mechanical fashion. Their habitation was dreary and there was no opportunity for social intercourse. There is a terrible familiarity in this description. It could be about prisoners, the mad, the depressed, or the abandoned old. It describes equally the grey men of Auschwitz and the forgotten babies of Rumania, the sad groups of hungry Ethiopians and the Cambodian refugees. These people ask, like the imprisoned Bonhoeffer:

> Who am I?
> Am I then all that which other men tell of?
> Or am I only what I know of myself,
> restless and longing and sick, like a bird in a cage,
> Struggling for breath, as though hands were compressing my throat,
> Yearning for colours, for flowers, for the voice of birds,
> thirsting for words of kindness, for neighbourliness,
> trembling with anger at despotisms and petty humiliation,
> tossing in expectation of great events,
> powerlessly trembling for friends at an infinite distance,
> weary and empty at praying, at thinking, at making,
> faint, and ready to say farewell to it all.
>
> Dietrich Bonhoeffer *Who am I?*

Brian Keenan, the Belfast schoolteacher released after four years' captivity in Beirut, spoke with devastating honesty of the psychological reality of being imprisoned, held hostage by cold, implacable gaolers:

> There's a silent, screaming slide
> into the bowels of ultimate despair.
> Hostage is a man hanging
> by his fingernails
> over the edge of chaos
> and feeling his fingers slowly straightening.
> Hostage is the humiliating stripping away
> of every sense and fibre
> of body mind and spirit
> that make you what you are.
> Hostage is a mutant creation,
> full of self loathing,
> guilt and death-wishing,
> but he's a man –

a unique and beautiful creation
of which these things are no part.[3]

This, then, is my understanding of the underworld and I believe it cannot be far from the ancient Jewish image of Sheol. It is small wonder, then, that the early Christians were excited at the rumours that the risen Christ had descended among the dead, that he had stormed the gates of hell and set the captives free.

It seems that the theological concept that Christ, in rising from the dead, had conquered death forever was illustrated by the early Christians as the victorious Messiah, the avenging God, physically breaking down the gates of hell and rescuing the spirits of the virtuous dead, Adam and Eve, the prophets and ancient fathers. The earliest description that I can find comes in the apocryphal Gospel of Nicodemus. It is not known who wrote this fascinating document but it is thought to have been written no later than the fourth century and to be based on a much older oral tradition.

It is here that we have the basis for the ancient concept of the Harrowing of Hell, so beloved of the early fathers of the Church and in Byzantine art and liturgy. The story goes like this:

Two sons of Simeon, the High Priest who had received the child Jesus in the temple, were raised from the dead after Jesus died. When they heard about this, the priests Annas and Caiaphas, and the Jewish elders Nicodemus, Joseph and Gamaliel went and found them, and brought them into Jerusalem, to the synagogue where they prevailed upon them to write down what they had seen and heard before they were released. The Gospel of Nicodemus, then, purports to be the testimony of Karinus and Leucius and this is the story they tell:

> Now when we were sat together with all our fathers in the deep, in the obscurity of darkness, all of a sudden there came a golden heat of the sun and a purple and royal light shining upon us. And immediately the father of the whole race of men, together with all the patriarchs and prophets rejoiced saying: This light is the author of everlasting light which did promise to send unto us his coeternal light. And Isaiah cried out and said: This is the light of the Father,

> even the Son of God, according as I prophesied when I lived upon the earth: The land of Zabilon and the land of Nepthalim beyond Jordon, of Galilee of the gentiles, the people that walked in darkness have seen a great light, and they that dwell in the land of the shadow of death, upon them did the light shine. And now it hath come and shone upon us that sit in death.[4]

I love this image of Isaiah suddenly understanding his own prophesy, like a man who realizes that his poetry has another and deeper meaning than that which he had initially intended. This particular prophesy read traditionally in our choral services is very precious to me for I have always identified the people who walked in darkness with the imprisoned and otherwise oppressed:

> The people that walked in darkness
> has seen a great light;
> on those who live in a land of deep shadow
> a light has shone.
> You have made their gladness greater,
> you have made their joy increase; . . .
>
> For all the footgear of battle,
> every cloak rolled in blood,
> is burnt,
> and consumed by fire.
>
> For there is a child born for us,
> a son given to us
> and dominion is laid on his shoulders;
> and this is the name they give him:
> Wonder-Counsellor, Mighty-God,
> Eternal-Father, Prince-of-Peace.[5]

After Isaiah comes the voice of old Simeon, the holy priest who received Jesus in the temple when he was presented as a baby. He too realizes that his prophesy has come true:

> Glorify ye the Lord Jesus Christ, the Son of God, for I received him in my hands in the temple when he was born a child, and being moved by the Holy Ghost I made confession and said unto him: Now have mine eyes seen thy salvation which thou hast prepared before the face of

all people, a light to lighten the Gentiles, and to be the glory of thy people Israel. And when they heard these things the whole multitude of the saints rejoiced yet more.

Apocryphal this Gospel may be, but the author has a wonderful knowledge and love of the Scriptures. He remembers the prophesy of another valiant old man, Zechariah, the father of John the Baptist who, when his speech returned, spoke prophetically of his son's mission as the man who was to prepare the way of the Lord, the Messiah.

And you, little child,
you shall be called the Prophet of the Most High,
for you will go before the Lord
to prepare the way for him.
To give his people knowledge of salvation
through the forgiveness of their sins;
this by the tender mercy of our God
who from on high will bring the rising Sun to visit us,
to give light to those who live
in darkness and the shadow of death,
and to guide our feet
into the way of peace.

The Benedictus[6]

After John the Baptist, Adam speaks and there is a great buzz of excitement among all the assembled patriarchs and prophets who have dwelt since death in Sheol, in this terrible no man's land of shadows.

Then comes a wonderful dialogue between Satan and Hades, the keeper of the underworld. Satan announces in triumph that he has persuaded the Jews to capture Jesus and put him to death and tells Hades to make ready to receive him. Hades, however, is appalled, for he has met Jesus before.

I adjure thee by thy strength and mine own that thou bring him not unto me. For at that time I, when I heard the command of his word, did quake and was overwhelmed with fear, and all my ministries with me were troubled. Neither could we keep Lazarus, but he like an eagle shaking himself leaped forth with all agility and swiftness and departed from us . . .

I love this image of Lazarus who I had always imagined stumbling slowly out of the tomb bursting out like an eagle, shaking himself and no doubt laughing in delight. It is a good image of resurrection!

Hades is not daft. He realizes at once that his prison will be quite unable to contain Jesus:

> wherefore now I know that that man which was able to do these things is a God strong in command and mighty in manhood, and that he is the saviour of mankind. And if thou bring him unto me he will set free all that are shut up in the hard prison and bound in chains by their sins that cannot be broken, and will bring them into the life of his godhead forever.

Alas for Hades, even as he protests, it is too late: 'suddenly there came a voice of thunder and a spiritual cry: Remove, O princes, your gates, and be ye lift up, ye everlasting doors, and the King of Glory shall come in.'

Hades panics and tells Satan to get out, and shouts to his ministers to bar the gates, 'lest we that hold captivity be taken captive'. By now, however, the prisoners are in revolt and they shout at Hades to open the gates.

Then, suddenly, they all hear it, a great voice of thunder saying: 'Remove, O princes, your gates, and be ye lift up ye doors of hell, and the King of Glory shall come in.' Then follows a dialogue echoing David's famous Psalm, 'Who is the King of Glory' and, then, there is a brilliant light and Christ appears: 'the Lord of majesty appeared in the form of a man and lightened the eternal darkness and brake the bonds that could not be loosed: and the succour of his everlasting might visited us that sat in the deep darkness of our transgressions and in the shadow of death of our sins.'

There follows an account of the terrified protestations of Hades and his ministers, but it is to no avail. 'Then did the King of Glory in his majesty trample upon death, and laid hold on Satan the prince and delivered him unto the power of Hell, and drew Adam to him unto his own brightness.'

And that, in its essence, is the story of the harrowing of hell, of the day when Christ descended into the underworld and, breaking down the bronze doors, stormed the prison and, trampling evil underfoot, emerged triumphant, leading all the prisoners out into the sunlight and up to paradise. It is a wonderful story and as I write it I imagine it as an opera with magnificent solos and choruses and glorious triumphant music.

Perhaps it has indeed been made into an opera or an oratorio, for the theme was a popular one in the mediaeval mystery plays.

That this story and the theology behind it were crucial to the early church we know from some of the earliest writing of the Church Fathers and from the plethora of wonderful icons depicting the scene with its traditional cast of Adam and Eve, David, John the Baptist and the prophet Isaiah. Indeed, it was my own encounter with such an icon that enthused me to undertake this search not only for the ancient teaching on the harrowing of hell but to see what light it might cast in our own dark world.

In what way, I wonder, has Christ broken the chains that bind El Salvador and its people? In what way have the deaths of Archbishop Romero, Rutilio Grande and the American missionaries harrowed the hell of that war-torn country? It would be naive to think that these deaths brought peace, for they did not. The killings continue, and indeed six Jesuit priests and the two women who kept house for them were among those brutally murdered in 1989. There is, however, a very real sense in which my Good Friday people have leaped eagle-like from the tomb. Archbishop Romero knew that it would happen: 'My life has been threatened many times. I have to confess that as a Christian I don't believe in death without resurrection. If they kill me, I will rise again in the Salvadoran people' (February 1980).

And rise again he did. Romero, the gentle Archbishop, is surely dead, but Romero the martyr, inspiration and hope of his people, is very much alive. Had they not killed him, he would, no doubt, have continued with his pastoral work and his denunciations of the killings, but his voice would have been largely confined to El Salvador. But they did kill him, and Romero is now a world figure, his life immortalized in a film and his words printed and reprinted to inspire a congregation way beyond his dreams.

And what of the missionaries, four quiet women whose days were spent in feeding and comforting a rag-tail bunch of refugees and orphans? They, too, have risen on wings as eagles, and have burst the bonds of political silence in the United States. El Salvador is now a key issue and the case of the murdered women a hot potato in Congress. It is no longer a simple matter to offer clandestine support to the Salvadoran regime because it happens to be politically convenient: questions are asked and quiet ex-ambassadors have found the courage to speak out on behalf of the missionaries and their work. And all this because three nuns and a lay missionary who, in life, were of no great consequence have sprung forth, in new life from the tomb which held them captive. Their dry bones, like those in Ezekiel's vision, have become clothed in life and have begun to dance. 'The hand of Yahweh was laid on me, and he carried me away by the spirit of Yahweh and set me down in the middle of a valley, a valley full of bones.'[7]

I think, at once, when I read this, not of an ancient Israelite cemetery but of the terrible mass graves of the people of Auschwitz or of those more recently uncovered in the Chilean desert. Hundreds of young men and women, missing for years, are suddenly being identified by the parents who mourn them, because the dry heat of the desert has preserved in recognizable form the jeans and shirts in which they were arrested.

Will their bones, too, be called forth, I wonder? The Lord said to Ezekiel: '"Son of man, can these bones live?" I said, "You know, Lord Yahweh". He said, "Prophesy over these bones." Say, "Dry bones, hear the word of Yahweh."' And the prophet spoke the word of God to the bones and the breath of life entered into them. They were clothed with flesh, sinew and skin, and, with a great clattering, they came to life again, a vast army of resurrected people. I believe that the dry bones in the Chilean desert have somehow been clothed with flesh and are, even as I write, harrowing the hell that was once Chile.

Poor Chile's sterile fields
Where no flowers grow.
Where beauty's withered.
Meadows of impaled liberty,
Fenced around with wire
Where no bird sings
to the machine guns' rattling crack of death.

Where the whining southern wind
carries the impotent shout of a race
in torment and the lament of a tribe
that have lost their Beloved.

Maria Bernales
Tres Alamos Concentration Camp
Santiago, Chile, 1975[8]

After seventeen years of oppression, Chile has broken her chains. There are no more detentions, no more torture centres and a commission of peace and reconciliation is investigating all the disappearances and deaths.

When I was in the grey detention camp of Tres Alamos, with five hundred captive men and women, prisoners spoke with confidence of the day they would be free. When I left I carried with me, written on the hem of my jeans, the poem I've just quoted, and its finale:

Gringa! God *is* love!
But never forget
that Chile is sobbing out her desolation.
Gringa! Go! Back to those
to whom you belong
and when the bells peal
Freedom's plangent ring
And when, across the air,
the high Andean winds
bring you the cry or laughter
of a happy child,
And you hear the mighty chorus of men and women
Singing of a liberty hard won,
Then, as one of us, come back
and join the endless chorus of the Free.

Maria Bernales

Today is the first time I have read Maria's poem since its prophesy has come true and I marvel at her faith. Perhaps she knew, better than I, the truth about death and resurrection.

And death shall have no dominion.
Dead men naked they shall all be one
with the man in the wind and the west moon,
When their bones are picked clean and the clean bones gone,

They shall have stars at elbow and foot;
Though they go mad they shall be sane,
Though they sink through the sea they shall rise again,
Though lovers be lost, love shall not;
And death shall have no dominion.

Dylan Thomas *And Death Shall Have No Dominion*

Lord of the living,
Lord of the dead:
be patient with your people.
Forgive us when we lose faith,
strengthen us when we lose hope,
give us a glimpse of your face,
that we may comfort your people.
We pray for the dying
and for those who weep.
Show them, O Lord, your mercy.

20

Great and Holy Saturday

Awake, sleeper!
I have not made you to be held a prisoner in the underworld.
Arise from the dead,
I am the life of the dead.

An Ancient Homily
for Holy Saturday

I never really understood Easter Saturday until I saw the icon of the harrowing of hell in the Irish monastery of Glenstal. Until then I had thought of the day that the Orthodox Christians call Great and Holy Saturday as a sort of bland sandwich filling between the dreariness of Good Friday and the radiance and joy of Easter Day. How, I wonder now, had I missed the power and the beauty of the Ancient Homily for Holy Saturday in spite of listening to it for nearly ten monastic Easters? Whatever the reason for my dullness of heart, the brilliance of an ancient Russian icon started me on a journey of discovery which was to lead me deep into the heart of the Orthodox liturgy and finally back to a much clearer understanding of my own tradition.

It happened like this: on a visit to Limerick I stayed in the Benedictine monastery of Glenstal hoping to find a little space to pray and to write the closing chapters of this book. As so often happens, my time became fragmented and my heart was not quiet enough to write so I tried to relax and enjoy the gracious monastic hospitality. As part of this hospitality I was taken to visit a small crypt chapel in which was displayed a gift to the monastery, a breathtaking collection of Russian icons.

I have always loved icons and have, for a number of years, used the Rublev Icon of the Trinity as a focus when I pray.

When I say I use it as a focus, I mean I gaze at the icon and the candle before it but am somehow focussed for depth far beyond the actual painting. I do not *think* about what I look at, just use it to still my heart and centre on God. I was planning, therefore, to look at these icons in the monastery crypt in the same way, but as our guide began to explain the pictures to us I found myself fascinated by what he said.

The icon we were looking at was of the *resurrection*, but it showed Christ's descent into hell. On the left was Adam, being led from the tomb by the hand, and also King David, John the Baptist and the prophet Isaiah. At Christ's feet were the gates of hell, and the instruments of torture being trampled on and destroyed. When we enquired what Adam and Isaiah were doing in hell he started to tell us the tale of Nicodemus' Gospel that I recounted in the previous chapter. Suddenly the whole story came alive for me. I could 'hear' Isaiah remembering his prophesy about the people that walked in darkness and I could sense David's mounting excitement as he realized the 'ancient doors' were about to open to admit 'the King of Glory'. More than anything, however, I stared at the instruments of torture. Here was something real, something I knew about, a link with my own life and with that of my Good Friday people. Suddenly I saw not Adam and the Fathers of the Church being rescued from hell, but my own people. If the risen Christ was trampling down the bronze gates and freeing the trapped souls in Hades, then surely he must have been there in exactly the same way for Ita and her friends trapped in that hideous death van on the Salvadoran hillside. I had always known that Christ was there, suffering with them, but I had never thought of him as risen, as Christ the valiant in war rescuing his people.

I found the idea enormously exciting and somehow infinitely more logical than a quiet and dignified transition from death to new life. Suddenly I saw resurrection as a magnificent explosion into joy and life and laughter, just as Lazarus leapt eagle-like from the tomb.

My excitement became barely containable and I pressed our guide with questions. Patiently, he explained all he could and when we returned to the guest-house presented me with a copy of Nicodemus' Gospel and a description of Hades. When I read the latter I knew I was right: that terrible world of shadows, of living and barely living, was not just an ancient mythological concept, not just a place which used to exist two thousand years ago, but it exists now, under all sorts of disguises. It is the prison of the depressed, of the political detainee, and the starving. It is wherever men are held hostage, in chains, suspended, terrified over the abyss, with their fingers slowly straightening.

And Christ, the King of Glory, is still the conqueror, still breaking down the bronze doors, still kicking the foul implements of torture back into the abyss where they belong.

I find it difficult to explain this insight without sounding foolish. It's not that I imagine Christ coming as a man waving his cross and physically assaulting devils, dictators and torturers. Of course not. It's something infinitely more mysterious. But the *imagery* has somehow given me an insight into the joy and wonder of Christ triumphant over sin and death.

It's a lovely idea, I thought, but is it 'true'? Does it hold water theologically, or am I falling into the age-old temptation of 'bending' the Scriptures to suit my own purposes? Determined to find an answer, I embarked forthwith upon a private theological investigation into the harrowing of hell and its relevance today, searching most especially for its relevance to my Good Friday people, men and women who are somehow 'called to suffering' and a messy, unquiet death.

I should remind the reader that I am not a theologian but a medical doctor and I work full-time in a maritime city whose bookshops are well stocked with treatises on marine engineering and biology but extremely low on patristics and spirituality! Limited therefore in both time and reference material, I set about reviewing the resources available to me and immediately summoned my friend Benedict, father of eight and carer of about twenty young schizophrenics, who is first and foremost an Orthodox priest. Ben is a wonderful reference person because not only is he well read and extremely articulate but he combines a rare enthusiasm with great patience. I put a handful of coins in the meter and switched him on. He waxed lyrical and I was entranced. It was as though the room darkened and I was transported in time and place to an ancient Russian church. It was Holy and Great Friday and Matins, the office of the Holy and Redeeming Passion of Our Lord Jesus Christ, was about to begin: It is dark and the people are gathering to hear the reading of the passion: the Service of the Twelve Gospels. While the candles are being given out, the priest sings:

> The glorious disciples were illumined at the supper during the washing of the feet, but ungodly Judas was darkened by the disease of avarice, and he delivered Thee, the righteous Judge, to lawless judges.

Then, the reading begins. The first is John 13 and the story of the Last Supper is told followed by antiphons recounting how the wretched Judas betrayed his master.

By the Second Gospel we have crossed the brook of Cedron and are standing impotently in the garden of Gethsemane, while Jesus is arrested. More antiphons follow, then more prayers – and suddenly there is a glimpse of light in the prayer to Mary: Mother of God.

> Hail Mother of God, who hast contained in thy womb Him whom the heavens cannot contain. Hail, Virgin whom the prophets preached: through thee Emmanuel has shone forth upon us. Hail Mother of Christ our God.

There we are, in the middle of the passion, being reminded that Jesus is Emmanuel, God with us, and that he is soon to break his chains.

In the Third Gospel, Jesus is interrogated, Peter denies him and the cock crows.

In the Fourth, Jesus stands before Pilate. They take him away and scourge him, and then he is brought before the crowd who are told, 'Behold your King'.

There are more prayers, then the antiphon and then, another shaft of light as Jesus says to the Jews:

> O my people, what have I done unto thee? Or wherein have I wearied thee?
> What have I done unto thee, and how has thou repaid me? Instead of manna thou hast given me gall, instead of water vinegar; instead of loving me, thou hast nailed me to the cross. I can endure no more. I shall call My Gentiles and they shall glorify Me with the Father and the Spirit; I shall bestow on them eternal life.

Even as he predicts his storming of hell, Jesus is led away to be crucified and the people sing:

Today He who hung upon the waters is hung upon the Cross
He who is King of the angels is arrayed in a crown of thorns
He who wraps the heavens in clouds is wrapped in the purple of mockery.
He who in Jordon set Adam free received blows upon his face.
The Bridegroom of the Church is transfixed with nails.
The Son of the Virgin is pierced with a spear.
We venerate Thy Passion, O Christ
Show us thy glorious Resurrection.

Jesus hangs on the cross dying but we are reminded again that this is the beginning, not the end:

> Today the veil of the temple is rent in twain, as a reproof against the transgressors; the sun hides its own rays seeing the Master crucified. *Antiphon 12*

Again and again we see it. Deep in the darkest moment of the passion the light forces its way under the door. True, it is Good Friday but it is also Great and Holy Saturday, Christ is dying but he is also rising.

> Thy Cross, O Lord, is life and resurrection to Thy people; and putting all our trust in it, we sing to Thee, our crucified God: have mercy upon us. *Antiphon 15*

It's as though the Church is continually reminding her people of the truth behind the passion, so that they may not lose heart. It is no accident that crucifixes in the Orthodox tradition bear, not the dejected figure of the moribund Jesus of Nazareth, but the triumphant Christ ready to spread his wings like the eagle.

As the wake continues we catch glimpses of a new theme: the marriage feast. Mary follows the procession to the cross with the other women and in her grief she cries out strangely:

> Where dost Thou go, my Child? Why dost Thou run so swiftly? Is there another wedding in Cana, and art Thou

> hastening there to turn the water into wine? Shall I go with Thee my Child, or shall I wait for Thee? Speak some word to me, O Word: do not pass me by in silence. Thou hast preserved my virginity, and Thou art my Son and God. Ikos.

Good Friday is a day of fast. There is no celebration of the liturgy, no distribution of hosts preconsecrated. No lunch is served to sustain the worshippers:

> on this day of the Crucifixion we eat nothing, according to the words of the Lord spoken to the Pharisees.
>
> 'The days will come, when the Bridegroom shall be taken from them, and then they shall fast.' But if, as frequently happens, anyone is weak and very old, and cannot keep the fast, let him be given bread and water after sunset.
>
> *The Lenten Triodion*

At around four o'clock the people reassemble for Vespers. There are more readings and psalms and a solemn veneration of the *Epitaphion*, an oblong piece of stiffened cloth on which is painted or embroidered the figure of the dead Christ laid out for burial. After Vespers comes Compline. Jesus is dead and all the liturgy is bursting with the grief of the Mother of God.

> 'In my arms I hold Thee as a corpse, O Loving Lord, who hast brought the dead to life; grievously is my heart wounded and I long to die with Thee, for I cannot bear to look upon Thee lifeless and without breath.
>
> 'O God supreme in love, O Lord all-merciful, I am filled with horror as I see Thee dishonoured, lifeless, without beauty, stripped and I weep as I hold Thee. Woe is me. I never thought to look upon Thee thus, my Son.
>
> 'O Word of God, hast Thou no word for thy hand maiden? Hast Thou no pity, O master, for Thy mother?' said the All-Pure, lamenting and weeping and kissing the sinless body of her Son.

At about the seventh hour of the night, at one o'clock in the morning, Matins of Holy Saturday begins. The priests stand in front of the *Epitaphion*, the icon of the dead Christ, and sing the funeral hymn, known as *the Praises* which are sung alternately with the verses of Psalm 118. Back and forth, the lines counterpoint each other:

> My soul has cleaved unto the dust: quicken Thou me according to Thy word. To earth has Thou come down, O Master, to save Adam: and not finding him on earth, Thou has descended into hell, seeking him there.

At last the burial hymn is over and the priest venerates the image of the dead Christ and then suddenly there is a change in the antiphons. It is as though everyone suddenly realizes that the tomb is soon to be empty.

> 'Why mingle ye sweet-smelling ointment with tears of pity, O ye women disciples?' cried the angel who shone as lightening within the tomb to the women bearing myrrh. 'Behold the tomb and rejoice: for the saviour has risen from the grave.'
>
> *Evlogitaria of the Resurrection*

What comes through very clearly at this juncture is the mystery of Christ's physical and spiritual presence. Physically, he is dead in the tomb, but mystically he is both with God in heaven and rescuing the captives from hell,

> O Lord my God, I will sing to Thee a funeral hymn, a song at thy burial: for by Thy burial Thou hast opened for me the gates of life, and by Thy death Thou hast slain death and hell.
>
> All things above and all beneath the earth quaked with fear at Thy death, as they beheld Thee, O my Saviour, upon thy throne on high and in the tomb below. For beyond our understanding Thou dost lie before our eyes, a corpse yet the very source of life.
>
> *Canticle One*

I love this spelling out of the mystery of death. I think in this context of the people standing around the dry grave on the Salvadoran hillside as the bodies of Ita Ford and her friends are dragged out, and I long for an angel, bright as day to say to them: 'Why mingle ye sweet-smelling ointment with tears of pity . . . Why count ye the living among the dead? . . . the time for lamentation is ended; weep not but tell the apostles of the Resurrection.'

There follows a series of nine canticles, each celebrating the mystery of the death and resurrection. We get another glimpse of the marriage theme in Canticle Six as Christ is likened to Jonah emerging after three days in the tomb of the whale's belly.

> Jonah was enclosed but not held fast in the belly of the whale; for, serving as a figure of Thee, who has suffered and was buried in the tomb, he leapt forth from the monster as from a bridal chamber and he called out to the watch: O ye who keep guard falsely and in vain, ye have forsaken your own mercy.

This image of Christ bursting forth from the tomb as a primitive bridegroom from his nuptial chamber is central to the Christian understanding of death and the mystical significance of the grave. Christ, like Lazarus, bursts forth with an eagle's energy as a lover would emerge in triumph from his tent to the expectant crowd bearing the evidence of the consummation of his marriage. Here we have the most mysterious and holy of all Christian symbolism: the grave as a marriage-bed where the dead are both mystically united with their Creator and born into new life.

The Orthodox liturgy of Holy Saturday finishes with Vespers during which there is much further reading of Scripture and singing of antiphons. Towards the close of the service the priests change their dark vestments of mourning into the white and silver of Easter.

It was only after I had made my way slowly through the glorious but marathon liturgy of the Orthodox Triodion that I came full circle back to the Roman rite, and in Matins of Holy Saturday rediscovered this Ancient Homily which celebrates the harrowing of hell.

> What is happening? Today there is a great silence over the earth, a great silence, and stillness, a great silence because the king sleeps; the earth was in terror and was still, because God slept in the flesh and raised up those who were sleeping from the ages. God has died in the flesh, and the underworld has trembled.
>
> Truly he goes to seek out our first parent like a lost

sheep; he wishes to visit those who sit in darkness and the shadow of death. He goes to free the prisoner Adam and his fellow prisoner Eve from their pains, he who is God and Adam's son.

The Lord goes in to them holding his victorious weapon, his cross. When Adam, the first created man, sees him, he strikes his breast in terror and calls out to all: 'My Lord be with you all.' And Christ in reply says to Adam: 'And with your spirit.' And grasping his hand he raises him up, saying: 'Awake O sleeper, and arise from the dead and Christ shall give you light.'

I am your God, who for your sake became your son, who for you and your descendants now speak and command with authority those in prison: 'Come forth', and those in darkness: 'Have light', and those who sleep 'arise'.

Here we have the familiar story from the Gospel of Nicodemus, the rescuing of Adam. But there is more:

I command you: Awake sleeper, I have not made you to be held a prisoner in the underworld. Arise from the dead. I am the life of the dead. Arise O man, work of my hands, arise, you who were fashioned in my image. Rise, let us go hence; for you in me and I in you, together we are one undivided person.

Here we have it clearly stated: we are not made for death and corruption but for union with God.

Here indeed is the tomb as marriage bed, as the place of consummation of the union of a man or woman with their God.

The cherubim throne has been prepared, the bearers are ready and waiting, the bridal chamber is in order, the food is provided, the everlasting houses and rooms are in readiness, the treasures of good things have been opened; the kingdom of heaven has been prepared before the ages!

An Ancient Homily
for Holy Saturday

We pray, O Lord,
for all who must soon face death,
whether by illness, old age or violence.
Strengthen them in their fear,
comfort them in their grief,
and give them some taste,
some inkling of the joy
you have prepared for them.

21

This is the Night

This is the night when Jesus Christ
broke the chains of death
and rose triumphant from the grave.
The power of this holy night
dispels all evil, washes guilt away,
restores lost innocence, brings mourners joy.
Night truly blessed when heaven is wedded
to earth
and man is reconciled with God!

The Exultet,
the Liturgy of the Easter Vigil

The more I think about it, the more I see the issue of the empty tomb as a red herring, a sort of chorus of sirens luring us away from our true course and on to the rocks of theological bickering and discord. Of course the question of who moved the stone and what exactly we mean when we say that Jesus rose *bodily* from the dead is fascinating but it is not central to our belief in the *resurrection* of Christ.

The questions 'how are dead people raised?' and 'what sort of body do they have when they come back?' are perennial ones and Paul had no patience with them.

> They are stupid questions. Whatever you sow in the ground has to die before it is given new life and the thing that you sow is not what is going to come; you sow a bare grain, say of wheat or something like that, and then God gives it the sort of body that he has chosen: each sort of seed gets its own sort of body . . . Then there are heavenly bodies and there are earthly bodies; but the heavenly bodies have

a beauty of their own and the earthly bodies a different one.[1]

The rising of Christ in the spirit, and whatever form his *new* body took, his descent among the dead and his harrowing of hell *are* central to our faith, for that is the cornerstone of our belief in a God who has power over evil and death. Even more important, and for me totally breath-taking, is the image of the wedding of earth with heaven, the union of frail human beings with their immortal unknowable God. *This* is the essence of our faith: the immortal, invisible God only wise, Yahweh, El Shaddai, the Ancient of Days who lives in light inaccessible, has somehow entered into his world, into his creatures and become united with them. This is such a mysterious, incredible state of affairs that we cannot cope with it, we are blinded, dazed and, lowering our gaze, search for something concrete to wrestle with, something like the mystery of the empty tomb. We rush about, examining the discarded shroud, looking behind the bushes, completely ignoring the patient angel who says, 'Why look among the dead for someone who is alive? He is not here; he has risen.'[2]

The Church, patient and exasperating mother of us all, does her best to explain the wonder and the mystery of Easter to us. Like a master detective she sets out each Easter night to reconstruct the events leading up to the victim's death and, having laid out all the clues before us, proceeds to explain their significance and how she arrived at her conclusion. Our great tragedy, it seems to me, is that we are often so familiar with the story that we become blind and deaf to the evidence and in so doing completely miss the truth. We are like people watching a familiar late-night movie: we know the story so we think we don't need to concentrate and our mind wanders or we drift off to sleep. For two and a half hours we drift in and out of consciousness and then, the lights go up and everyone sings the Allelulia. We rejoice. Lent is over, Christ is risen and we go off to drink cocoa and eat Easter eggs. Happy Easter. Christ is risen. He is risen indeed. But what does it mean?

Let me turn the video back.

It is night. Darkness covers the earth. It is the beginning of time and chaos reigns. The black waters rage and the earth is a formless void. People and priests stand silently around an unlit fire: we are waiting for the beginning of life. The Spirit of God broods expectantly over the silent chaos and, suddenly, there is a spark of light. The spark catches and there is a flame: it is the New Fire, the light of God, suddenly bursting into flame on earth. Our hearts leap: THIS IS THE NIGHT!

The priest blesses the fire:

> O God who by thy Son, the corner-stone, didst convey to thy faithful the fire of thy glory: sanctify this new fire, produced from the flint and destined for our service. Grant us through this Easter festival to be so inflamed with heavenly desires, that we may come with minds made pure to the festival of thy undying radiance: through the same Christ our Lord.
>
> *Prayer for the Blessing of the New Fire*

This prayer is taken from the old Roman rite. The modern form has been somewhat watered down: 'Make this new fire holy, and inflame us with new hope. Purify our minds by this Easter celebration, and bring us one day to the feast of eternal light.'

I wonder who decided to substitute 'inflame us with a new hope' for 'grant us to be so inflamed with heavenly desires'? Perhaps some enthusiastic liturgist decided that these words from the old Roman liturgy were a bit over the top for modern Christians and that 'hope' was a more suitable sentiment than 'desire'. While I see that the new translation is shorter and pithier I think it actually misses the point. Whoever wrote that ancient prayer said exactly what he meant: he was asking God that the Easter festival should inflame people's hearts with a mad burning passion for their God, that they would become so possessed, so taken over by love that they would never again fall from grace and so would come, in death, to union with the God of the dazzling dark, of the undying radiance. It's not quite the same as hoping to be a guest at a festival of light, jolly as that will be.

After the Blessing of the New Fire comes the Blessing of the Incense to be inserted into the paschal candle. In my modern missal, this ceremony is optional, so we are in danger of missing a vital clue to the mystery of Easter.

Even when this blessing is performed it may escape all but those closest to the celebrant, for it is a fiddly business carried out only by the light of the bonfire. The celebrant takes five grains of incense which represent the five wounds of Christ and, in blessing them, recalls the atoning power of Christ's suffering and death. Without these wounds, without this death, we would not be here tonight.

The grains of incense, the five wounds, are now inserted into the paschal candle which is to represent the risen Christ. The celebrant cuts a cross in the wax of the candle with a stylus, and traces the Greek letter alpha above the cross and the letter omega below it while saying:

Christ yesterday and today
the beginning and the end,
Alpha
and Omega;
all time belongs to him,
and all the ages;
to him be glory and power,
through every age and forever.

The grains of incense are then inserted while the priest says: 'By his holy and glorious wounds, may Christ our Lord guard us and keep us.' The priest then lights the candle from the new fire, the light of the Word springs forth from the loins of his Father, the Eternal Light. The candle is lifted high and carried into the darkened church, the waiting world, as the deacon sings, first softly and then even more loudly, 'Lumen Christi, The Light of Christ' and the people say politely, formally, 'Thanks be to God!' when they should be throwing their caps in the air and dancing a jig, shouting like lunatics, 'He's coming, he's coming, the people that waited in darkness have seen a great light! Emmanuel, God is with us.'

The people light their candles and settle down while the deacon clears his throat to begin the Easter proclamation, the Exultet.

It is truly right
that with full hearts and minds and voices
we should praise the unseen God, the all powerful Father,
and his only Son, our Lord Jesus Christ.

For Christ has ransomed us with his blood,
and paid for us the price of Adam's sin
to our eternal Father!

Then come the marvellously immediate statements in which the key Jewish events: their rescue from Egypt, and safe conduct through the Red Sea and the desert are mysteriously brought together with Christ's death and his triumphal rising. We find we are celebrating all these things at once, that THIS IS THE NIGHT when God is present among his people:

This is the night when first you saved our fathers:
you freed the people of Israel from their slavery
and led them dry shod through the sea.
This is the night when the pillar of fire
destroyed the darkness of sin!
This is the night when Christians everywhere,
washed clean from sin
and freed from all defilement,
are restored to grace and grow together in holiness.
This is the night when Jesus Christ
broke the chains of death
and rose triumphant from the grave.

Then comes the Pauline message: without all this we would have been done for:

What good would life have been to us,
had Christ not come as our Redeemer?
The power of this holy night
dispels all evil, washes guilt away,
restores lost innocence, brings mourners joy;
it casts out hatred, brings us peace and humbles earthly pride.

Here we are plunged once more into mystery. How are we to understand this passage, for alas we do not see hatred cast out in the here and now? But wait: perhaps we do, but it is not an all at once phenomenon, rather the brave struggling of a fragile plant to take root in an arid land. This past year has brought us undreamed of peace, especially in Eastern Europe. A year ago this month I stood in East Berlin looking up at the Brandenburg Gate and the great Wall. And now, the wall is down and I hold a small piece of it in my hand, brought as a gift from a medical student amazed at his freedom to backpack around Europe. Now the green blade riseth, but we must wait for the harvest.

Once again we have the marriage theme:

> Night truly blessed when heaven is wedded to earth
> and man is reconciled with God.

Slowly the dark church fills with light as candle after candle is lit. I always love this moment, both the soft light and the strange shadows on the roof and walls of the church and the amazing symbolism of tiny lights, together overcoming the darkness.

> The Easter candle is offered to God:
> Accept this Easter candle,
> a flame divided but undimmed,
> a pillar of fire that glows to the honour of God
>
> Let it mingle with the lights of heaven
> and continue bravely burning
> to dispel the darkness of this night!
>
> May the Morning Star which never sets find this flame still burning.
> Christ, that Morning Star who came back from the dead,
> and shed his peaceful light on all mankind,
> your son who lives and reigns forever and ever.
>
> *The Exultet,*
> *the Liturgy of the Easter Vigil*

After the Exultet comes the Liturgy of the Word, a reading of lessons from Old and New Testament. The priest explains:

> Dear friends in Christ,
> we have begun our solemn vigil.
> Let us now listen attentively to the word of God,
> recalling how he saved his people throughout history
> and, in the fullness of time,
> sent his own Son to be our Redeemer.

How difficult it is, of course, to listen attentively to eight long Scriptural readings all of which are full of complex symbolism that takes a while to understand. I suspect, alas, that it is impossible to appreciate these readings without a certain amount of homework, reading and re-reading of the passages, following up the cross references and searching out the themes. If one does embark upon such an exploration, however, one enters a world of stunning beauty and logic.

Meanwhile, however, let me try to unlock first some of the secrets of these Easter Vigil readings. (To do it thoroughly is way beyond me and would fill a book in its own right.)

In this series of readings there are two main themes: the creation of the world (hence the reading from the first chapter of Genesis) and the creation of God's people, our spiritual ancestors, the people of Israel. These themes run in parallel, and interwoven in them are a number of other themes, Water, Covenant, Baptism and New Birth. Let me explain.

God creates the world out of a shapeless void: the waters of chaos. By breathing over these waters he tames them and gives them life and fecundity. To inhabit this new world he creates a man and a woman, Adam and Eve. Adam is the father of the whole human race and, alas for us, he sins and is driven out of the garden. Adam's race then populates the earth and, because of his fallen nature, they make a mess of things and God in his anger decides to wipe them out and start again, using a small remnant of his creation, Noah and his family and their animals.

All this is told in Genesis chapters 5, 6, 7 and 8 (omitted from the new Roman rite). After the flood God makes a covenant – the first of many – with his people and promises that never again will he destroy them.

God then sets out to fashion his people and he sends Abraham on a journey into the unknown. (This story is much beloved by missionaries who see themselves as following God's call in faith. It is the essence of Christian discipleship.) Abraham, the father of God's own people, is very precious to him and God, as is his wont, decides to test him yet again. He asks him to offer Isaac, his only beloved son, as a holocaust. This is in some ways a terrible and mysterious story, the basis for the ritual presentation of the first-born, the first-fruits, of the people of Israel to God. The important thing is that the offering is not sacrificed but redeemed, bought back. The ancient Fathers of the Church saw the sacrifice of Isaac as a prefiguring of the passion of Jesus.

After the Isaac story comes the wonderful drama of the crossing of the Red Sea. The Israelites are rescued by God from the hand of their enemies, saved from the chaos of the waters of destruction. They sing to the Lord in their delight:

> I will sing to the Lord, glorious his triumph!
> Horse and rider he has thrown into the sea!
> The Lord is my strength, my song, my salvation.
> This is my God and I extol him,
> my father's God and I give him praise.[3]

Here we have a prefiguring of the warrior Christ who overcomes the chaos of darkness and hell.

In the next reading from Isaiah 54:4–14 we have a wonderful image of the forgiveness and faithfulness of God. The people of Israel have fallen from grace yet again and the prophet likens them to a faithless wife whose husband, having abandoned her in a rage, now comes to take her back. It is a passage of amazing tenderness which leaves us in no doubt that Yahweh is a God of mercy not vengeance:

> Do not be afraid, you will not be put to shame,
> do not be dismayed, you will not be disgraced;
> for you will forget the shame of your youth
> and no longer remember the curse of your widowhood.
> For now your creator will be your husband,
> his name, Yahweh Sabaoth;
> Your redeemer will be the Holy One of Israel,
> he is called the God of the whole earth.
> Yes, like a forsaken wife, distressed in spirit,
> Yahweh calls you back.
> Does a man cast off the wife of his youth?
> says your God.

Here we have with startling clarity the marriage symbolism which runs throughout the whole of the Easter liturgy and is to emerge again with great power in the ceremony of the Blessing of the Font.

This passage leaves us with a restating of the covenant:

> for the mountains may depart,
> the hills be shaken,
> but my love for you will never leave you

and my covenant of peace with you will never be shaken,
says Yahweh who takes pity on you.[4]

In the next reading, Isaiah 55:1–11, which is a continuation of this passage from Isaiah we return to the water theme, but this time it is not the waters of chaos but the waters of life.

O come to the water all you who are thirsty;
though you have no money, come!

The waters of life are free, for God has given himself freely to his people. The water of life is the Word of God which gives life to the earth which is his creation.

Yes, as the rain and the snow come down from the heavens and do not return without watering the earth, making it yield and giving growth to provide seed for the sower and bread for the eating, so the word that goes from my mouth does not return to me empty, without carrying out my will and succeeding in what it was sent to do.[5]

Water, light, fire, thunder, all the familiar images which evoke in primitive and modern people alike a sense of the power behind the universe, are used in the Scriptures to speak of God. In the reading from the prophet Baruch we have the ancient theme of the Wisdom of God, that creative power which brings life into being and holds it, miraculously, in existence. The prophet rebukes the people of Israel for having forsaken the 'fountain of wisdom', the waters of life, and reminds them of the mind-blowing truth of just who their God is. Yahweh is no small time deity but the God of Gods, he who fashioned the universe and at whose command the lights of heaven come and go.

. . . he has set the earth firm for ever
and filled it with four-footed beasts,
he sends the light – and it goes,
he recalls it – and trembling it obeys;
the stars shine joyfully at their set times:
when he calls them, they answer, 'Here we are';
they gladly shine for their creator.
It is he who is our God,
no other can compare with him.[6]

God has revealed this to his people, it is written in their

Scriptures. The prophet implores Jacob (the people of Israel) to return to the light, not to throw away their birthright as God's chosen people.

> This is the book of the commandments of God,
> the Law that stands for ever;
> those who keep her live,
> those who desert her die.
> Turn back, Jacob, seize her,
> in her radiance make your way to light:
> do not yield your glory to another,
> your privilege to a people not your own.
> Israel, blessed are we:
> what pleases God has been revealed to us.[7]

I find it amazing to contrast the different faces of God, the different way he reveals himself (herself, themselves!) and the different way we respond to that revelation. In particular I love the paradox of the unknown mysterious creator God and the God whose relationship to his people, individually and collectively, is that of the lover. We see this latter face of God in the marriage symbolism, in Isaiah and Hosea, in the Song of Songs and in many of the Psalms:

> Like the deer that yearns
> for running streams,
> so my soul is yearning
> for you, my God.
> My soul is thirsting for God
> the God of my life;
> when can I enter and see
> the face of God?[8]

At last, we emerge from the Old Testament readings to the New, and find, in Paul's letter to the Romans, the drawing together of the golden threads and the summary of the Easter message:

> . . . when we were baptised in Christ Jesus we were baptised in his death; in other words, when we were baptised we went into the tomb with him and joined him in death, so that as Christ was raised from the dead by the Father's glory, we too might live a new life.[9]

Here we have it: the merging of the imagery of baptism and death, of union with God and the emergence of new life from old. Baptism is not just the pouring of water over the head of a squalling infant, it is the going down with Christ into the waters of chaos, into the tomb, and rising, united with him from those same waters which he has transformed into the waters of life. Even as I write these words I know, as Paul must have known, that he was writing of a mystery, hard to understand, hard to accept.

The readings are followed by another ceremony, the blessing of the baptismal font and its water, preparing it for the celebration of the sacrament of baptism. I had no idea, until I embarked upon this search, of the richness of the symbolism and imagery of the Easter Vigil and in particular of the blessing of the font. This symbolism which has been largely deleted from the new liturgy is clearly spelled out in the old.

The baptismal font, the receptacle for the water used in baptism, represents both the grave into which we descend and the womb of the Church. The paschal candle, the icon of the risen Christ, is lowered into the font, and by this entering the grave, the womb, the waters of chaos he renders it fruitful.

> May this water, prepared for the rebirth of human beings, be rendered fruitful by the secret inpouring of his divine power; may a heavenly offspring, conceived in holiness and re-born into a new creation, come forth from the stainless womb of this divine font; and may all, however distinguished by age in time or sex in body, be brought forth into one new infancy by the motherhood of grace. Be gone then every unclean spirit at thy bidding, Lord; be gone all wickedness and satanic wiles. Let no power of opposition intrude here or spread its snares about this place, or creep into it by stealth, or taint it by its poison.
>
> *Prayer for the Blessing of the Font,*
> *Old Roman Liturgy*

This image of Christ's sanctifying of the waters of chaos speaks powerfully to me, for as my Good Friday people are plunged into the black chaotic waters of death, so those waters are made fruitful. The deaths of the martyrs of El Salvador mysteriously transform the chaos of evil into the waters of grace and life. As Tertullian knew: 'The blood of the martyrs is the seed of the faith'.

After the blessing of the font, and after any baptism, the people are called upon to renew their Baptismal Promises:

> Dear Friends,
> through the paschal mystery
> we have been buried with Christ in baptism,
> So that we may rise with him to a new life.
> Now that we have completed our Lenten observance,
> let us renew the promises we made in baptism
> when we rejected Satan and his works,
> and promised to serve God faithfully
> in his holy church.
> Do you reject Satan?
> And all his works?
> And all his empty promises?
> Do you believe in God, the Father Almighty,
> creator of heaven and earth?
> Do you believe in Jesus Christ, his only Son,
> our Lord?
> Who was born of the Virgin Mary,
> was crucified, died and was buried, rose
> from the dead,
> and is now seated at the right hand
> of the Father?
> Do you believe in the Holy Spirit,
> the holy Catholic Church, the communion of
> saints,
> the forgiveness of sins, the resurrection
> of the body,
> and life everlasting.

The people holding their candles (now getting dangerously low!) firmly declare 'I do'.

What an amazing ceremony that renewal of vows is. On the surface it is so formal, so dry, so legal, like a court statement or a marriage contract. Yet, what an immensity of faith and joy and pain it covers: as we stand there we protest our belief in an all-powerful mysterious unknowable God, who made the heavens and the earth and we hold, deep in our hearts, the wonderful, terrifying knowledge that he loves us, desires us, calls us to him. Like the deer that yearns, so our souls thirst for the living God: and that thirst drives us out into the highways and byways to care for his people. It drives us to denounce injustice, to feed the hungry, to clothe the naked and to shelter the homeless poor. Just where that love will take us we never know, but remember the Good Friday people and we tremble in our shoes.

We tremble because we are afraid that we too may be called to powerlessness, to follow Jesus along the road to Calvary. We fear the pain, the weariness, the humiliation, and the loss, but most of all we fear that we may not be equal to what is asked of us. It's all right for THEM – we say; they're special, holy, stronger, braver, somehow different from us, a people set apart. But are they so very different, I wonder? I don't think so. I believe that we are all, all, potentially Good Friday people. We are all frail, earthen vessels who may, should the potter choose, be fashioned in his image and for his own mysterious purposes. He chooses the weak and makes them strong in bearing witness. Their strength is his. The light they cast is his. And we, all we have to do is remember that his love is better than life itself, and say 'YES'.

I finish with Carla's song: a prayer mysteriously answered:

> Waters of Mountains – waters of God
> cleanse us, renew us so shabbily shod.
> Rios de Chile, streams of burnt snow
> melt us, tow us beyond friend or foe.
> Currents so fast, pools deep and clear
> tune us, quiet our hearts still to hear.
> Lord of the river, God of the stream
> teach us Your song, our dryness redeem.
>
> Carla Piette
> El Salvador, 1980

Appendix

And so we must begin to live again,
We of the damaged bodies
And assaulted minds.
Starting from scratch with the rubble of our lives
And picking up the dust
Of dreams once dreamt.

And we stand there, naked in our vulnerability,
Proud of starting over, fighting back,
But full of weak humility
At the awesomeness of the task.

We, without a future,
Safe, defined, delivered
Now salute you God.
Knowing that nothing is safe,
Secure, inviolable here.
Except you,
And even that eludes our minds at times.
And we hate you
As we love you,
And our anger is as strong
As our pain,
Our grief is deep as oceans,
And our need as great as mountains.

So, as we take our first few steps forward
Into the abyss of the future,
We would pray for
Courage to go places for the first time
And just be there.
Courage to become what we have

Not been before
And accept it,
And bravery to look deep
Within our souls to find
New ways.

We did not want it easy God,
But we did not contemplate
That it would be quite this hard,
This long, this lonely.

So, if we are to be turned inside out,
And upside down,
With even our pockets shaken,
Just to check what's rattling
And left behind,
We pray that you will keep faith with us,
And we with you,
Holding our hands as we weep,
Giving us strength to continue,
And showing us beacons
Along the way
To becoming new.

We are not fighting you God,
Even if it feels like it,
But we need your help and company,
As we struggle on.
Fighting back
And starting over.

Anna McKenzie

References

Chapter 1: Introducing Good Friday People

1. Isa. 53:1–5.
2. Anna Carrigan, *Salvador Witness* (Ballantine Books).
3. Daniel Berrigan, *The Bride.*

Chapter 3: Called to Powerlessness

1. Luke 9:23.
2. Luke 2:41ff.
3. Matt. 10:17f.
4. Anna Carrigan, *op. cit.*, p. 55.
5. Ps. 62:3.
6. *ibid.*, p. 59.
7. *ibid.*, p. 64.
8. Jer. 20:7.
9. From Oscar Romero's speech at the ceremony in Louvain, 1980, when he received the Nobel Prize for Peace. Quoted by Placido Erdozain in *Archbishop Romero* (Lutterworth Press), p. 73.
10. *ibid.*

Chapter 4: Towards Jerusalem

1. William J. O'Malley, *The Voice of Blood* (Orbis Books), p. 12.
2. *ibid.*
3. *ibid.*
4. *ibid.*
5. Luke 11:42f.
6. Isa. 9:1.
7. Isa. 61:1.
8. *The Gospel at Solintiname* (Orbis Books), vol. 2, p. 3.
9. O'Malley, *op. cit.*, p. 34.
10. *ibid.*, p. 39.

11. *ibid.*
12. *ibid.*, p. 45.
13. Jon Sobrino, *Archbishop Romero. Memories and Reflections* (Orbis Books), p. 7.

Chapter 5: We Without a Future

1. Luke 9:58.
2. Dietrich Bonhoeffer, *Letters and Papers from Prison* (SCM Press Ltd).
3. Judith Noone, *The Same Fate as the Poor* (Maryknoll Sisters, New York).
4. Ezek. 11:19.
5. *ibid.*

Chapter 6: A Party in Bethany

1. John 11:44.
2. John 11:54.
3. Luke 6:37f.

Chapter 7: Last Suppers

1. Archbishop Romero, Homily for 17 February 1980.
2. Anna Carrigan, *op. cit.*, p. 234.
3. Matt. 20:18f.
4. Ita Ford, Report to the PANISA Regional Assembly, 22 November 1980, quoted in *The Same Fate as the Poor.*
5. Gwen Vendley, administrator of Maryknoll Lay Mission Program, quoted in *Salvador Witness*, p. 210.
6. *ibid.*, p. 212.
7. John 13:33–4.

Chapter 8: Dark Night

1. Mark 14:33.
2. Judith Noone, *op. cit.*, p. 44.
3. *ibid.*, p. 45.
4. *ibid.*, p. 129.

Chapter 10: The Way of Dispossession

1. Job 42:1–6.
2. Psalm 62:3.
3. James Doherty, *It's Never the Same* (Veritas Publications).
4. *ibid.*, p. 18.
5. *ibid.*, p. 19.
6. *ibid.*, p. 20.
7. *ibid.*, p. 23.
8. *ibid.*
9. *ibid.*, p. 29.
10. *ibid.*

Chapter 11: Torture

1. Joan Jara, *Victor. An Unfinished Song* (Jonathan Cape).
2. *ibid.*

Chapter 12: Crucify Him, Crucify Him

1. Matt. 26:59–66.
2. John 8:3–11.
3. Matt. 25:14–30.

Chapter 14: Pockets Shaken

1. *The Dream of the Rood*, trans. E. Colledge, in *A Christian's Prayer Book* (Jackman).

Chapter 15: Last Words

1. Isa. 52:13, 14.
2. Joan Jara, *op. cit.*
3. Archbishop Romero, from an interview in a Mexican newspaper, February 1980.
4. Matt. 27:45–7.
5. Ps. 22:25–6.
6. Ps. 22:1–2.

Chapter 16: Good Friday

1. John 12:23–54.
2. Brockman, *Romero, A Life* (Orbis Books).
3. John 19:25–7.
4. Wisd. 3:1.

Chapter 17: Darkness over the Land

1. Matt. 27:45.
2. Gospel of Peter V. 15–20.
3. Matt. 27:51–3.
4. Exod. 24:12–18.
5. Exod. 25:22.
6. Exod. 26:31.
7. Exod. 40:34.
8. Exod. 40:36–8.
9. 1 Kings 6:19.
10. 1 Kings 6:12–13.
11. 1 Kings 9:3, 6–7.
12. Heb. 9:11.
13. Heb. 9:26.
14. Heb. 4:15.
15. Heb. 4:16.
16. Job 38–41.
17. Job 42:3, 6.
18. Annie Dillard, *Holy the Firm* (Harper & Row Inc.).

Chapter 18: The Day of the Lord

1. Isa. 2:10–12, c. 740 BC.
2. Zeph. 1:14–16, 18.
3. 1 Pet. 3:18f.
4. Matt. 16:18f.
5. 1 Cor. 15:12–14, 16–19.
6. Hab. 3:3–6.
7. Hab. 3:9f.
8. Hab. 3:11f.
9. Hab. 3:17–19.
10. Rom 8:35–9.
11. 1 Cor. 15:55.

Chapter 19: The Harrowing of Hell

1. *New Larousse Encyclopaedia of Mythology.*
2. Gen. 37:34f.
3. Words spoken at a press interview on 30 August 1990.
4. The Gospel of Nicodemus, *The Apocryphal New Testament*, trans. Montague Rhodes James (OUP).
5. Isa. 9:1–2, 4–6.
6. Luke 1:76–9.
7. Ezek. 37:1.

8. Trans. Trader Faulkner, October 1984.

Chapter 21: This is the Night

1. 1 Cor. 15:36–8, 40.
2. Luke 24:5.
3. Exod. 15:1f.
4. Isa. 54:10.
5. Isa. 55:10f.
6. Baruch 3:32–6.
7. Baruch 4:1–4.
8. Ps. 41:1–2.
9. Rom. 6:3–4.